Reade

"I truly enjoyed reading the second book of the Modica's adventures while settling into Lucca, Italy after receiving their dual citizenship. The pages give you a true sense of how everyday life is versus vacationing in Italy. Having visited myself several of the sites and villages they mention, their words brought back that magical feeling that being in Italy brings me. The book provides so many practical details of their personal experiences while relocating to a new country, unafraid of pointing out the lows as well as the highs of the process. Their experience provides the encouragement that once hard to fathom dreams can actually with determination come true."
—**Barbara Winshurst**

"Not everyone gets to fulfill a major life dream, but Ilene and Gary get to fulfill that dream and more. Their first book, *Our Italian Journey*, was an adventure of looking throughout Italy for 'their perfect place to live'. This book, *When Your Heart Finds Its Home*, is about finding that place and making it 'their home'. You are introduced to a lot of their friends, places, and their Italian discoveries in the book which makes for a wonderful read.
—**Frank Shackleford**

"Life gives you the most beautiful gifts and it has given us Ilene and Gary Modica's captivating tale of their journey to finding their forever home in Italy. When Your Heart Finds its Home is a lovely, intimate, and charming memoir of Italian life and travel. Italy is generally regarded as having the most inevitable lifestyle. The way Ilene and Gary have described the scenery, the people, and their experiences surely support this and make me want to follow in their footsteps. How have they made it entirely possible for me to be homesick for a place I've never been? When Your Heart Finds Its Home, did just that. Excellent, beautifully written, this is a book I'll keep and reread time and again." —**Susan Lauciello**

"Continue the Italian adventure with Gary and Ilene that began in their first book 'Our Italian Journey' only now, join them as they find their heart's true home in the town of Lucca, Italy. Heartfelt and heartwarming, Ilene and Gary recount the journey that took them back to Italy- although much later than they had hoped. However, once there, they pick up right where they left off.

When I read 'When Your Heart Finds Its Home,' I felt as if I were sharing a glass of wine with Gary and Ilene as they told me the story of their experiences in Italy! And one thing that stands out in all of their stories is not only their love for Italy but their love for people! Family, friends, Italians, or anyone, Gary and Ilene place people first, and that is so evident in this book! When you are finished reading it, you feel as if you know both Italy and them a little bit better!

The other thing about Gary & Ilene that comes across in their book is that they never take their lifestyle for granted. They clearly cherish every moment that their lifestyle allows them to experience. And they want to share that experience with us. In their conversational and humorous style, they paint such a vivid picture of life in Italy that I feel as if I'm right there with them. They make Italy accessible to all of us. Whether you may be lucky enough to take the leap and do what they did or not, you will enjoy 'living the dream' through their eyes and their anecdotes. Once again, thank you Gary & Ilene for sharing your adventure with us!"
—Diane Selkregg

When Your Heart Finds Its Home

The Journey Continues

The Journey Continues

By Ilene and Gary Modica

Published in Phoenix, Arizona

When Your Heart Finds Its Home

Publisher's Note: *When Your Heart Finds Its Home* describes the authors' experiences while moving and living in Italy, and reflects their experiences and opinions. To protect privacy, some individual names have been changed. This is a continuation of their first book, *Our Italian Journey.*

Cover photo of Porta San Gervasio and back photo of Guinigi Tower were taken by JoAn Ferguson in Lucca, Italy, August 2022.

Cover designed by Ilene Modica

ISBN: 978 1 7353761 1 0

Library of Congress Control Number: 2022915110

Published in the United States
by Boston Harbor Press LLC
Phoenix, Arizona

ouritalianjourney@gmail.com

ஓ Dedication ல

For our children,
Melanie, Jared, Jacklyn, Allyson

and grandchildren,
Aidan, Noah, Avery, Cooper, Gianna, Brooklynn,
Evrett, Kyla, Logan

You are in our thoughts and prayers every day.
Thank you for understanding about our dream
to live in Italy.

Contents

Introduction

Ilene

Many of us go through life searching for… "something." Some may never quite find what they're looking for. Others may not be aware of what that "something" even looks like. Is something missing? Are we sure? Should we consider listening to that little voice, telling, nagging, prompting us, for… something more? In such cases, a bit of soul searching is often necessary. That little voice could linger as a desire, a dream, or crazier yet—the meaning or purpose of your life. Your happiness more than likely won't come to you—but it can come from you. I truly believe each heart beats differently and for different reasons. Mind you, I'm not referring to your heart's rhythm—but what we each search for in life. What would bring satisfaction, joy, or contentment to your life? What might that look like… for you?

ଔ

For Gary and me, it became the hunt for our "perfect" Italian town. Now, this took some doing because our search—and our love for a country five thousand plus miles away from our home in Phoenix, Arizona—took quite a few trips and much exploration.

This pursuit launched a lot of fun and excitement—even so, might our expectations have been set too high? Could we leave family behind to create a completely new chapter in our lives—living far away from family and friends… at this stage of our lives? Could we endure months-long separations from our kids and grandkids—especially during holidays and birthdays? Would it be possible to endure these tugs to our heartstrings and emotions? Were we selfish for wanting this new life for ourselves?

The Journey

Ilene

We went to Italy for the first time in 2010, long before Gary ever thought of trying to obtain, dual citizenship. We planned this vacation like any other, for a typical two-week duration. It became one of those zany itineraries trying to jam-pack everything into the days allotted without killing ourselves. Like most, we only had so much vacation time saved up from our jobs.

We arrived in Venice and took the train to way too many cities and towns. The flight home from this very first trip to Italy turned out quite thought-provoking. Sitting on the plane, I could see Gary's mind working on something privately. His silence spoke volumes. After settling in for the long flight back to the States, we both turned and faced one another—we each revealed we didn't want the vacation to end. I'm sure everyone experiences this sense of emptiness or letdown at the end of a great vacation. However, this time was different. Plain and simple—we didn't want to leave Italy. While in Italy, we both sensed we were "home." Home in a country we'd never been to before. How was that even possible? It was insane… crazy. Nevertheless, our feelings were real—we couldn't deny or ignore them. Neither one of us.

ᘓ

By the time we returned home to Arizona, we had already begun planning our next trip to Italy. Like many people who've had the pleasure of visiting Italy, one trip to this beautiful country was not enough, and we weren't any different. We took three more, dazzling trips to "the boot" between 2012 and 2017. We were thrilled with each trip we took and always eager to return. Yet for Gary, that "something" kept gnawing at him about his genealogy and whether he could become an Italian citizen. His grandfather was born in Sicily and when he emigrated to America in 1909, he never became an American citizen. *Bingo.* The lightbulb went on.

ᘓ

Gary

By far, one of our most frequently asked questions through the years has been, "Why go through the hassle of obtaining citizenship with another country—Italy?" The benefits are many and straightforward. Let's reveal some for you.

First, one of the most significant benefits of Italian dual citizenship is the ability to travel, live, and work in any… *any* of the twenty-six member states of the Schengen Area. The Schengen Agreement, signed in June 1985 in Schengen, Luxembourg, established the abolition of internal border controls among many, though not all, European countries. Fortunately for us, Italy is a member of the Schengen Area. We can live for however long we'd like in Italy or any other member country. We can freely work, redefining our retirement status if we wanted to, without acquiring a Work Visa. These types of visas usually come with time limitations and are very specific in the details.

Furthermore, the subject of the education system is by far, more affordable than in the United States. Italy is home to some of the oldest universities in the world offering high-quality education with low tuition fees. Imagine attending a school whose alumni list included Leonardo da Vinci, Michelangelo, or Niccolò Machiavelli.

For us, being retired, the US healthcare system became extremely expensive. With Ilene retiring early and under sixty-five years old, we could only afford catastrophic healthcare for years. With an Italian National Healthcare card, we would have secure access to one of the best and most affordable healthcare systems in the world. It's our understanding, that Italy's quality healthcare system is among the top five rated in the world, while the United States ranks toward the middle of the list. This, of course, depends on the source you use to acquire this information.

Another benefit is being able to take part in numerous tax deductions when purchasing a home in Italy. There are many rules and regulations when it comes to this topic, but the advantages are many. As they can change frequently, you would need to research the current guidelines on an official site on the Internet if you wanted specific information.

Even so, one of the most alluring reasons people choose to become Italian citizens inevitably amounts to the benefits you pass along to your children. If you're already an Italian national, you pass this right to your children and grandchildren—even if they aren't yet born. Future generations can enjoy all the same benefits. You pass an unbroken link of advantage, privilege, and opportunity to them. It's a gift that continues to give. In our case, thank you Pop, my paternal grandfather.

☙

Ilene

Like most immigrants of the nineteenth and early twentieth centuries, the reason countless Italians left their beloved country was to escape poverty, harsh conditions, and to provide their children with a better life. A life that a substantial number imagined was available to them in America, where the streets were supposedly paved with gold. Gary's grandparents left Italy not because they didn't love their country—far from it. They brought their Italian heritage, traditions, and culture to their new country to start a better life. To enhance life for them and their children, and generations to come. The Italians, perhaps more than any other immigrant wave in

America, succeeded beyond their wildest dreams—according to YouGovAmerica, (Linley Sanders, *These are America's Favorite Foods From Around the World,* March 12, 2019) Italian cuisine is the number one favorite food (eighty-eight percent) in the United States today, if not the world. Becoming an Italian citizen would bring Gary's heritage full circle and honor his Pop in a way he could not have imagined all those years before.

ထ

At any rate, you know our story. Gary's quest to acquire Italian citizenship was formidable and the cost substantial. Patience was essential, as time wasn't something under our control, but completely in the hands of the Italian government. *Oh boy...* Gary's application for Italian citizenship was the culmination of the roller coaster ride of our lives. This journey took nine days short of three years through the Los Angeles Italian Consulate. Once Gary's citizenship was approved, I automatically received mine. The "1983 Italian Law," abolished automatic Italian citizenship through marriage on April 27, 1983, however, those married prior to this date are excluded from this ruling. Due to the fact we were married in 1980, before this law took effect, I was automatically granted the honor of Italian citizenship at the time Gary became an Italian citizen. At long last! After all that time, effort, and focus, we now had some decisions to make. What would we do with this little, maroon-colored Italian passport we finally obtained?

ထ

Our story continued with a year of traveling through Italy—a year of spontaneity, adventure, and happiness. As we embarked on a completely new chapter in our lives, we decided to document our journey to help others with their own personal pilgrimages. The work culminated in our first book, *Our Italian Journey.* An unexpected memoir of our first year living like Italians through Italy.

We now also had a new mission—we needed to find our new home. Our new mission: finding our "special place" in a country where every village offers gorgeous scenery, fabulous food, and charming people. Had it been everything we'd hoped for—just the one-year adventure? Where would our hearts find its final home?

Return to Italy in 2021

Ilene

Like thousands of others, our plans to travel in 2020 didn't materialize and, unfortunately, returning to Italy in May of 2020 didn't occur. The reason, of course, was COVID-19, which literally and figuratively stopped… everything on Earth. To say that the last two and a half years has been challenging for every one of us is the understatement of the century. First and foremost, if you, dear reader, lost a loved one, friend, or colleague, Gary and I offer our heartfelt condolences for your loss. Those who did not suffer personal loss of life, likely had children or grandchildren who suffered through remote learning, lacking important and quality time with teachers and classmates. I often wonder if our young grandchildren will remember this pandemic. Will some remember not attending school, or missed gatherings with friends for sleepovers, and birthday parties? Will they remember wearing a facemask everywhere they went? My heart broke for our oldest grandson, Aidan, who graduated high school without any hoopla. I'm curious how this pandemic will end up recorded in the history books. We've all been through a rollercoaster ride of emotions. I can easily recall that my emotions ran the gamut from sadness—to fear—to anger.

ᴄᴓ

As Italian citizens, we could return to Italy at the beginning of 2021. Citizens could always return to Italy; the issue became finding a flight. Gary and I talked about it—discussing it often, wondering… should we go? Should we stay with our children until the worst of the pandemic subsides—will it ever?

ᴄᴓ

When we return to Arizona, we enjoy staying at Melanie and Jerry's home. Melanie is Gary's daughter from his first marriage. She and her husband own a lovely home with a spare room including a private bathroom in Arizona. It's referred to as the "Italy" room. Remember, back when we "sold it all," this also meant our living accommodations too. I feel very close to Melanie, and think of her as my daughter. I may not have given birth to her, but deep love and respect rank first and foremost in our relationship. However, after five months of disrupting their home life, we thought we should figure out other living quarters. No one knew how long this pandemic would cause travel restrictions, and we didn't wish to become a burden and overstay our welcome. We looked at a few apartments to buy, but prices were substantial, and the selection in our preferred locations turned out to be less than perfect. We searched but couldn't find anything reasonable that would allow ongoing travel to Italy. Our thought process at the time—to live six months in both countries. In the end, we just couldn't stretch our limited budget to accommodate this lifestyle.

ᴄᴓ

Our daughter Jacklyn and her husband, Andy, purchased a new home in Phoenix in 2019 during our year adventure through Italy. It came with a unique and interesting feature—a feature not currently in use. The west side of their home included a recreational vehicle pad, including full hookups. The previous homeowners already installed the independent sewer and electric connections.

This vacant space between them and their neighbors presented an area to conduct bicycle races and play hopscotch. Their invitation was offered and we became neighbors—very close neighbors. The purchase of a motor home became our solution to the pandemic.

It turned out, many benefits presented themselves to this living arrangement. The absolute best perk? The little knocks on our door when our grandchildren fancied a visit. Cooper, nine years old at the time, Gianna, six, and Evrett five, were always a welcome surprise. We loved when a visit would turn into a discovery of what new snacks we bought (with them in mind) the last time we went grocery shopping. Movie night and sleepovers always bloomed into a jubilant adventure. I'm sure every grandparent knows this feeling, this love. In the morning after breakfast, we would return them to their parents. Another of the great benefits of being a grandparent.

☙

With the heat of the summer, the convenience of using their beautiful, unusually deep, built-in pool also became a big plus. On a workday, Gary's routine remained the same. He would come home from working at the PGA Tour Superstore in Glendale and quickly change into his bathing suit, enjoying a quick dip before dinner. Chilled Lambrusco wine became the choice of beverage during the summer kept cold in our Yeti sip-it wine glasses while enjoying the pool. The lids kept the pool water out as well as the inevitable chance of spillage from their three dogs pacing frantically around the perimeter. The most fun of all, certainly occurred when the kids joined us. These three resembled fish after years of swimming lessons.

Occasionally, I would make the announcement, "Nana would appreciate her hair not getting wet." It never turned out well.

A pitfall of being a grandparent? Being given the arduous task of telling them it was time to get out of the pool and dry off.

Barbequing on our originally owned grill also became a nice benefit. When we sold it all—Jacklyn and Andy became the recipient of Gary's six-burner pride and joy. Gary even mastered making risotto and pasta sauce, not just grilled items, so as not to heat our little motorhome.

☙

We bought the recreational vehicle to explore the United States while not being able to travel overseas. Boy, did this American adventure distort, pivot, swivel, and swirl into something completely different than we expected. We only left our daughter Jacklyn's driveway twice. Well, two times for adventures. However, both times we ventured only about 110 miles each trip to go to a campsite still open but with minor restrictions because of the pandemic.

On the first trip, we went to Cottonwood and the second to Sedona. Both are beautiful places in northern Arizona. Both with family and grandchildren. Nevertheless, it was as far as we could go. All the state parks we wanted to finally visit began closing one by one. There went the other reason for buying a motorhome, to explore places in the States we'd never trekked before. Our desire to reconnect with nature came to a screaming halt. Heartbroken, we finally decided to sell our brand-new beauty within the year.

☙

Our yearning to return to Italy remained strong. After all, we were now citizens, and our emotions were being pulled toward that country we loved. Besides, we didn't go through the citizenship process to stay in the States and only dream about Italy. We started looking into the current regulations for travel. We wanted to resume our Italian journey.

Requirements and procedures changed almost daily back in September 2020. A telephone call to the Italian Consulate in Los Angeles confirmed we could travel to Italy because of our citizenship status, but… we would need to follow tons of regulations. Gary combed the Internet, finding only a few flights still functioning and flying into Italy. We allowed ourselves to elevate our hopes, just slightly.

The consulate informed us we should monitor the updates on the Ministry of Health website as amendments to these regulations occurred weekly, sometimes even daily if they involved extensive changes. Considering the facts and keeping them in mind, we rebooked our flights to arrive in Rome on April 1, 2021. We kept our fingers crossed that April Fools' Day would not forecast any difficulty with our travel plans. *Primo aprile,* April first would give the pandemic situation six months to improve and hopefully make our return to Italy easier. How naive we continued to be when it came to Italy, and especially this scenario.

ᴕ

Originally, we both agreed to return to Arezzo. We love this medieval town in eastern Tuscany but, we found out the apartment where we previously stayed in 2019, was currently occupied by a resident and not available to rent. Searching the Internet, we just couldn't find anything quite as nice as Marcello's apartment.

After a conversation over a nice bottle of red wine, we unanimously decided on the town of Lucca in the western part of Tuscany. We would stay in one location for seven months, unlike our last adventure. If travel restrictions opened, it would result in a good "home base" for more exploring. In all our travels, we've yet to venture into the Piedmont region. Lucca's location would make traveling to this area very easy. This region is the second largest in Italy and is well-known for its truffles and famous wines. Need I say more?

ᴕ

We know everyone has opinions and beliefs about taking the vaccine and we respect this. For us, after some back and forth, we decided to receive the COVID vaccine before we traveled to Italy. It seemed easier to acquire the vaccine in the States as we'd read Europe experienced difficulty securing vaccines, especially Italy.

Unfortunately, at the time, I wasn't technically eligible to receive the vaccine because I was too young at the time. With the help of Gary's daughter, Melanie, she secured Gary's online appointment. Our strategic plan… for me to accompany him to his appointment, and perhaps (with luck) secure the vaccine even though I was under the age of sixty-five, the requirement at that time.

Arriving at State Farm Stadium in Phoenix for Gary's appointment, we were shocked at the well-organized system developed for accommodating these appointments. Truly astonished a city, *our city,* could carry out such precision. To us, Phoenix wasn't at the cutting edge. Arriving at the check-in station, we inquired about the possibility of me receiving the vaccine as well. The two volunteers working at this spot informed us "no shows" occurred every day, and I would be able to register as a "walk-in patient." Able to receive the vaccination shot as well, we both let out a sigh of relief. Securing the shots at the same time would benefit us both. What's the saying? Misery loves company. That's us. It's kind of weird we do so many things together. Our friends laugh at us, but we are a package deal. I guess we are truly, two peas in a pod.

☙

Italian Ministry of Health:

All of Italy will be declared a "red" zone from March 26-April 6

Gary constantly checked the Italian Ministry website for updates. As luck would have it, just days before our flight on March 31, a new health proclamation arose. We had a gut feeling that something would happen because of the Easter holiday. The strategy thus far was to stop travel and large gatherings for this holiday—to regulate the movement of its citizens to prohibit further spread of the virus. Italy devised a color system corresponding to risk scenarios for which specific restrictive measures were foreseen. These color indicators signified the number of cases in a region. When the Ministry of Health made a region "red," the number of COVID cases reported stood high and travel was not allowed in or out of the specific region. The colors, orange, yellow, and white, signified varying levels of restrictions that weren't as severe. White represented the lowest cases being reported. This did not derail us and even though it wasn't needed to enter Italy, we both took the COVID PCR test forty-eight hours before our flight. Once in Italy, we would follow the mandates to take a COVID test shortly after landing.

ɞ

When we arrived at Sky Harbor Airport in Phoenix, we noticed far fewer travelers. Of course, being five o'clock in the morning might have some bearing on this but, the bottom line—the airport remained extremely empty. While waiting at the gate, seats started filling up fast. *Were all these people traveling for the Easter holiday?* I removed some hand sanitizer from my pocketbook and offered some to Gary. I'm surprised so many people were traveling, especially now. The news reported most, if not all airlines encountered issues filling flights and it remained a big problem. Not that day, seats around the check-in podium were filled, and people stood in every possible open area. Our flight wound up being like a sardine can—packed. At the time, I became a little concerned, to say the least.

ɞ

The highlight of this trip consisted of making our way to the Dallas/Fort Worth International Terminal, our stopover before the final flight into Rome. We were extremely excited for this leg of the journey because Brett, whom we've mentioned several times in our previous book, our daughter Ally's significant other, gifted us the upgrade on this flight to business class. We'd never flown first class or experienced sitting in a business "pod" before. Our friends shared several stellar stories of life outside of coach with us, increasing my anticipation.

Selfishly, I must admit, I was looking forward to this flight for the opportunity to board the airplane before anyone else. Our tickets—Group One. I looked around the waiting area once in Dallas Fort Worth, and there were only a handful of people milling around the gate. This flight, by no means, would reach maximum capacity—not by a long shot.

A short ten minutes before boarding we heard an announcement. The American Airlines attendant announced all passengers on the flight to Rome must come to the desk. She instructed us to fill out two forms—the same two forms we previously filled out on the website, except these included a QR code for the airlines. So, it became a matter of just transcribing the same information but onto their forms. Busy filling out the documents for entry to Italy, we heard the announcement boarding of Group One. Both my papers completed I jumped up and gathered my things but Gary was still writing. I tend to write fast and Gary…he's quite the opposite. I glanced to see several people are already boarding the plane and I waited—tapping my foot, waiting as patiently as I could for Gary to finish filling out his papers.

As we finally entered the plane, we were shocked that there were only about a dozen other people on the flight, and two were in business class with us. The airline would certainly lose money on this flight. Our attendant, Scott showed us our seats. In the past, we've only passed through the business section on the way back to our seats in coach. I always envied the legroom and the chance to lay down comfortably on an airplane. These pod seats recline into flat beds—a sheer pleasure for an eleven-hour flight.

Scott had sensed my excitement and gave me an inquisitive look. I revealed to him this would be our very first time flying in business class. He smiled back, understanding my emotion. He shortly arrived with two glasses of Prosecco, welcoming us aboard with a faux leather pouch filled with a toothbrush, toothpaste, mouthwash, socks, and an eyepatch. Slippers, pillows, and blankets, all sealed in plastic were also presented. *Very impressive, I thought to myself.* It became quite an experience with Gary sitting on the other side of a sliding window. We resembled two police cars pulled over on the side of the road facing opposite directions. Just not relishing any donuts.

After we settled in, Scott handed us dinner menus including the wine list. Who knew business class was like dining in a restaurant? The combination of the comfortable pods and excellent service far exceeded our expectations. It was an international flight we will never forget. I'm not sure I'll ever be able to return to coach. Ultimately, I don't expect this idea to sit well with Gary.

☙

We experienced quite an eerie feeling while exiting the plane and making our way to customs. Hardly anyone existed in Rome's Fiumicino airport, normally an incredibly busy place. It looked like a ghost town from the wild west. A large dust bunny rolled down the corridor ahead of me causing me to think of the western frontier and tumbleweeds. Certainly, it wasn't big but because the corridors stood so empty, it had been easily visible to me. We saw just a handful of people other than the few on the flight with us. Complete silence filled the corridors. I recall reading somewhere silence is the loudest sound in the universe because it's the only thing that makes you stop and look around. I did just that. The intense silence permeated the space, not even music played from the speakers in the corridors.

It took us just a snap of a finger to arrive in the customs area and we walked right up to the customs booth. We offered the agent our travel papers and, without being asked, we handed her our beautiful, maroon-colored, still relatively new, Italian passports. The precious little books that evaded us for so long while acquiring our dual citizenship. Our prized possessions. Done and through customs in less than five minutes and we were off to the baggage area. Following the signs, smiles began to emerge on both our faces when we spotted both pieces of luggage, arriving safe and sound. It's always a good feeling and I'm sure, a fear amongst all travelers.

☙

Briefly, we walked around to find the place to score our COVID swab test but were unable to find one. With no one around to ask, we headed to catch the Leonardo Express. This train connects Fiumicino Airport to Roma Termini, Rome's central train station. Even though our new luggage was lighter than those on our previous year-long trip, they were still too heavy and cumbersome. Have we not learned to pack lighter? Soon, I regretted using a carry-on over my shoulder. Note to self for future travel, stick with something that has wheels.

☙

Arriving at the Leonardo Express area, and still not finding any testing sites, we bought our train tickets and decided to test once we arrived in Lucca. Everything we read indicated we were permitted forty-eight hours to take our test once arriving in Italy. I took the luggage to an open seating area while Gary bought our train tickets to Lucca.

I just started settling in and getting comfortable when moments later Gary called to me "Ilene," in a singing type of voice and I noticed he was waving me over. *Swell…what now, I thought?* I maneuvered both large pieces of luggage and carry-ons and made my way to where he stood in front of the ticket office.

"She needs your passport," Gary informed me.

We've never needed to show passports before, but Gary realized, she must need to verify we're citizens before issuing our train tickets. After paying EUR 99,20 we waited for the train to arrive on track one.

As the train approached, we headed for the sliding glass entry door where we must scan our tickets. *Had this been here before?* I don't recall seeing this barrier the last time we were in Rome's airport. Apart from this, what's noticeably different about this trip… a police officer stood positioned at this entry point taking everyone's temperature before being allowed to board the train. How COVID has changed our lives. All our lives. I must say, I became a little concerned because I'm quite overheated at this point in the trip, and feeling a bit clammy and dehydrated from the entire traveling process. I prayed, hoping the police officer didn't notice that I looked a bit dreadful. With fingers crossed, thankfully he let me pass without a second thought or any fuss.

Once on the train, Gary took a seat across from me and I smiled at him with a wink. We are here. We are home and it felt wonderful. No words were needed; he knew exactly what I was thinking. I'm an emotional person—just ask Gary or any of our children. Even one of our grandchildren could tell you about "Nana's tears." A sentimental commercial comes on the television with a baby or a dog and I'm weeping… and don't get me started on chick flicks. I've always worn my heart on my sleeve. As I watched Gary's eyes scan the train, I fought to hold back the tears of joy. My heart soared. We settled in for the four-and-a-half-hour, give or take, train trip from Fiumicino Airport to Lucca.

ଓ

After changing trains in Roma Termini to Pisa, we noticed the train acquired quite a few more passengers than expected. I noticed small pieces of luggage in various colors stowed in the overhead racks and assumed people were traveling to visit family and friends for the Easter holiday. Gary thought this to be quite odd because the Ministry of Health already declared all of Italy a "red" zone for travel restrictions during the holiday. These travelers gave every indication of heading home like us, or maybe there were just ignoring the COVID travel mandate?

On this train, Gary's assigned seat had been located across the aisle from me, facing in the same direction. From my seat and side of the train, I could see the Tyrrhenian Sea as we went speeding by. On this local train, we experienced quite a few stops.

At the Civitavecchia station, Gary reminded me, "This was where we were supposed to meet Joanie and John to begin the cruise." At one time, we had considered the possibility of returning to the States in October with our friends Joanie and John, who are also from Phoenix.

As I looked out the window, I caught a glimpse of several cruise ships docked. As cruise ships were a challenging way to travel during COVID, no one appeared to be traveling anywhere via a cruise right now. Thinking about how empty our last flight remained, and seeing all these cruise ships docked and empty, brought to reality how this pandemic has truly changed everyone's lives. The passengers who will not board those ships. The crew members who suffer from not working, some probably losing their jobs. The empty docks with no ships arriving at their ports. It goes on and on. It truly blows my mind the snowball effects this pandemic has caused—certainly in the travel industry. Will we ever know the entire truth about it?

ଓ

The Trenitalia manager in his dark navy suit with red trim came by checking tickets bringing me back to the moment, *"Biglietti,"* he said. He scanned our tickets by the QR code and continued down the train. I admired his shiny, recently buffed *nero,* black shoes. I watched him forge ahead down the aisle, but my eyes noticed something different, something new. Red arrow stickers affixed on the floor of the train symbolized which direction to walk. Although, I noticed no one heeding the notification. I began to wonder… when we arrive in Pisa, should we follow this indicator? Concerned, I made a mental note to monitor others as they left the train for their stop, figuring we would just follow the masses. This red strip, along with some large round stickers adhered on several train seats represented new additions because of the pandemic. Keeping a distance, the seat label indicated the particular seat must remain empty. Even in Italian, I understood. There were several of them strategically scattered throughout the train car. Even on the cement train platforms, large, round green standing notification stickers appeared everywhere and indicators on which way to ascend or descend on a flight of stairs.

☙

This leg of the journey, from Rome to Pisa took three hours and twenty minutes. As we sat back and relaxed, I took a few photos out the window. Around the Follonica stop, I spotted Isola d'Elba, a Tuscan Island out in the distance. Gary informed me that Napoleon was exiled to Elba after his crushing defeat at Waterloo. I rely on Gary for historical facts and information. The things he remembers blows my mind. As a happily married wife of forty-two years, too bad he doesn't remember things I ask him to do—but that is an entirely different story. I would love to visit Elba in the coming months. Italians love this island getaway and I want to find out more about it. This particular island, along with Sardinia are two we haven't visited and are high on the list when summer arrives.

☙

I realize I intended to work on a blog post while on this train trip or at least some Italian vocabulary words and phrases. I knew I should take out my laptop and at least give the impression of being productive, but I was tired, and just relaxing and gazing out the window became my quest for the day. I occasionally glanced over at Gary, and his eyes were shut, I did the same.

Pulling into the station in Livorno, I recall that Gary and I visited this town before. The view from the train was beautiful, but if I recall correctly, we couldn't find a restaurant open to enjoy a seafood *pranzo*, lunch. That day turned out to be a disappointment. Bear in mind, that we've learned throughout our travels, that one unsatisfying trip to a city shouldn't define it. Many things could have been a factor that day. Perhaps it might have been an Italian holiday we weren't aware of, who knows? Nevertheless, the point I'm trying to make—always give a town another chance, and we will return to Livorno. We gave Bari another opportunity and it surprised us. We changed our opinion one hundred and eighty degrees from our first visit.

Arriving in Pisa, we just missed the train to Lucca. While gathering our thoughts on the platform, two police, *Polizia di Stato,* approached us asking to see our documents. At first, I took out our train tickets but realized he wanted to see our travel documents for COVID. He looked at both our papers, reviewing each of them slowly. It's always at times like this I feel a little antsy. Satisfied, he nodded and returned the papers to us. I let out a quiet sigh of relief. We watched and noticed they asked everyone on the platform for travel documents. Those without forms were given the proper papers to fill out at once. I glanced over at Gary and gave him my "look," head tilt and all. We were compliant and knew these travel documents existed—a necessity to travel throughout Italy. We were good citizens, I thought without patting myself on the back.

ଓ

Gary went to find out the next train choice for Lucca. When he returned from viewing the *Solari* board, telling me we need to hang out and wait over two hours, I'm not satisfied. The lighted digital boards at train stations are named after the Italian display manufacturer, Solari di Udine. Our phones didn't show a Wi-Fi connection, so we were unable to contact our apartment owner informing him of our change in arrival time. Gary checked inside the station and found no Wi-Fi there either. Another deep sigh.

ↄ

Normally, we would buy Italian SIM cards at the airport upon arrival. Still, it meant we must put our "American" phone numbers on hold with our carrier in the United States. This used to cost us about USD 40.00 a month for both of us. Consequently, we each would obtain Italian numbers at a cost of about EUR 20,00 a month for both our phones.

While on this subject, we've often wondered why it cost so little for cellular service in Italy versus the States. The technology isn't any different. I can't figure out the discrepancy and have never received an adequate response when asking US wireless carriers about the cost difference. It's crazy, but so I digress. On this trip, things are different as Brett has added us to his International Plan with T-Mobile. Somehow, though, we haven't figured out why the Wi-Fi hasn't kicked in.

ↄ

Being very tired and not happy with the waiting scenario, I give Gary a dismissive gesture and head to the customer service agent in the main terminal. From our book and blog posts you know this means down a flight of stairs, through the tunnel under the tracks, and up the stairs to the main platform. It's a great deal of exercise, especially for those who don't do much on a regular basis. Did I mention, as luck would have it, the elevator was under repair on our platform? Yes… we lugged those heavy suckers up and down stairs—again. Travel can be exhausting.

ↄ

Arriving at the customer service counter, I inquired about the next train to Lucca. The woman pointed, indicating the train on platform one—just in front of us would leave at any moment and stop in Lucca. *Ahh...* I run to tell Gary and gather our luggage. I found Gary waiting in the tunnel.

"Hurry Gary, I found a train leaving now and stopping in Lucca!"

We piled into the small elevator at the main platform and arrived at street level. Rolling my luggage at a quick clip I spotted the customer service agent I spoke with earlier with her arms resting on the platform railing. I pointed to the train, and she shook her head in agreement.

I shouted out to her, *"Grazie Mille,"* and boarded the train with Gary right behind me.

Finding two available seats, I questioned Gary, "Did you not ask someone?"

In response to my question, I received raised eyebrows and a puppy dog look, and I didn't need to say anymore. I gather he didn't. What's with men and asking for directions?

By this point in the day, I'd overheated again and thirsty, quickly realizing I hadn't had anything to drink all day. We've traveled this train route before, and I pointed out to Gary a glimpse of the Leaning Tower of Pisa as we passed by. Down to the last leg, we know it's only about another thirty minutes before we arrive at our final destination. Our home for seven months. The thought brought a slight grin to my face.

cs

Arriving in Lucca, we were familiar with the town and headed for the *Cathedral di San Martino or Duomo di Lucca.* A *duomo* is an Italian term for a church built to serve as a cathedral. Our apartment was a few steps to the next piazza. Arriving in Piazza San Giovanni, we headed for our *verdi*, green-colored door. Our Airbnb owner greeted us and brought us into the ground-floor apartment. Thank goodness no stairs. I just don't think I could've done anymore at that point in the day. Showing us around, we were completely satisfied with the apartment.

We took a moment and assessed the kitchen contents, listing the basic things we would need to purchase right away. We decided before completely relaxing, and both hungry, that a quick trip to the nearest grocery store was in order. I pulled out my phone and found directions to PAM. The streets were unnervingly empty as we followed the blinking blue dot on my GPS. Occasionally *biciclette,* bicycles passed and just a handful of people were on the streets—all wearing masks as mandated by the Italian Ministry. Essentials obtained, we went back to the apartment. Realizing we had plenty of time to secure the proper COVID tests the next day, we ate and crashed for the night. Both exhausted, we woke up seventeen hours later. Seriously, we must have been tired! Who sleeps that long?

☙

Getting our COVID tests done became the mission for the day in order to maintain compliance with Italian law. As we headed inside the *farmacia*, pharmacy we handed the pharmacist our Codice Fiscale cards, equivalent to Social Security cards in the States, and paid EUR 44,00 for both our tests.

A young man in a white hazmat suit came into the pharmacy and indicated we needed to follow him out to the tent. As we entered the temporary tent outside the pharmacy, somehow, I had been elected to go first. He overheard us speaking and tried in his best English to explain the procedure.

I asked if we could take photos, and he agreed. He asked me a few questions and began unwrapping the swabbing sticks and testing equipment. He stood and told me to lift my head and sit still. When I told him, "Just don't fall forward," he laughed, and although I don't think he quite understood me, he precisely told me, "We make everyone cry." A burst of shared laughter exploded between all of us.

It wasn't a pleasant experience and different from the swab test we received in Phoenix several days prior. In Phoenix, the woman just swabbed around the inside tip of our nose. No, this gentleman went quite far up the nasal cavity, and I closed my eyes and imagined eating a large cone of gelato to take my mind off it. *Stracciatella*, chocolate chip—my favorite. Once finished, he swabbed the long stick on the test kit and told me I must wait ten minutes.

Meanwhile, it was Gary's turn. We switched places and now I took photos and videos of Gary's procedure. I noticed that he, too, closed his eyes, but I never asked him what he had been thinking about. Probably not gelato.

While waiting for Gary's COVID test results, mine returned negative. A few moments later we received Gary's results as well, which were also negative for COVID. "Mr. Hazmat" walked us back into the pharmacy where we each received a printed paper showing negative results. We thanked him and headed back inside the Renaissance wall to our apartment.

I understand the requirement to obtain the test. On the walk back to the apartment, we discussed the urgency of figuring out the Italian healthcare system. We were looking for a long-term rental or home to purchase in Italy. Although the EUR 44,00 cost wasn't extreme, I don't think as citizens with a *Tessera Sanitaria* card, we would need to pay such an amount. Gary puts it on his list of things to do.

Primavera, Spring

(March 21 - June 20)

ঌ New Best Friends ঌ

Gary

After being in Lucca for a month, Ilene received a message from a couple from Virginia, who saw one of our blog posts on social media. They also live in Lucca. Gianna and Giacomo are ex-pats using Italian-sounding names because their American names are difficult to pronounce. Gianna and her husband would like to meet for *caffè,* coffee at a *café* in Piazza San Michele.

ଓ

Since the Italian word *caffè*, is often confused with *café*, the place where this drink is served, let me explain the difference between these two words right from the beginning. Throughout this book, we will refer to a "coffee shop" or "coffeehouse," a place to acquire the dark, complex brewed drink that's prepared from roasted coffee beans as a "*café.*" In Italy, this place is often referred to as a bar. By no means are we trying to teach Italian in this book, but since we are living in Italy, it's the proper way to describe this establishment. It's a well-known fact that Italians love their *caffè.* The pronunciation [kaf-feh] refers to the drink itself. Italians created a culture surrounding this drink that's unparalleled in any other place in the world.

ᏣᏕ

Of course, we agreed to meet them at Turanodot Café, centrally located inside the Renaissance walls of the historic center. We arrived early as we were still on "American time." Honestly, I still can't do the Italian late thing.

We all sat down and ordered *colazione,* breakfast. After introducing ourselves, we promptly started asking them questions. They informed us they arrived in Lucca just days before the COVID lockdown. They explained their experience of life in Lucca during the pandemic and how they managed to gather what they needed for their elective residency to stay in Italy. We loved their story. We explained our situation as dual citizens and told them we'd be in Lucca until the end of October when we would return to Phoenix, Arizona.

Gianna told us about a gentleman who helps ex-pats meander through the bureaucracy to obtain a *Tessera Sanitaria* (medical card), *Carta D'Identita* (residency card), bank account, and the transfer of utilities if needed. His name is Tony, known to all in Lucca by many names. "Tony the Guy," "Tony the Navigator," or "Tony the Fixer." Of course, what we didn't realize at the time—we would need his services too. He is an ex-pat relocation specialist aiding newcomers with the brutal process of setting up life in Italy. Tony's the answer to all ex-pats' fears in Lucca trying to brave the bureaucracy alone.

We liked Gianna and Giacomo instantly. After finishing our *caffè,* we took a stroll through the cobblestone streets. We slowly ambled while they graciously pointed out several of their favorite shops and hangouts. It became a behind-the-scenes type of tour, and we treasured the special touch.

Ending up in front of their apartment, they invited us inside. It's in an amazing palazzo on the main street of town. Their apartment is on the top floor with stunning 360-degree views of the city of Lucca from their room referred to as an *altana,* a *Lucchesi* word for tower. Views of the beautiful mosaic San Frediano church, the Guinigi and *duomo* towers, and people walking on the wall, took my breath away. Views of the mountains just outside of Lucca were stunning.

Gianna expressed to us her love of photography. Birds are a favorite subject of hers to photograph, and as she said this, three seagulls swooped right in front of us and landed on their roof, just above our heads. Ilene ducked as she thought they appeared to fly right into the open window. Giacomo and I laughed out loud. With their mosquito screens opened, Ilene and I take several panoramic videos and photos of the reddish-orange rooftops of Lucca. From this height, photos of the Guinigi Tower turned out to be spectacular. The photos of this tower that our cellphones captured appeared to be so close, you'd think we used a drone. Gianna told us we must return to view the magnificent sunsets they enjoy most evenings. They've made this apartment their own and it's beautiful. With air kisses, we plan to meet them again soon.

☙

After our get-together, we headed back to our apartment. Ilene, without hesitation, turned to me and said, "I think we found our perfect Italian town."

Of course, she meant Lucca, and I couldn't agree with her more. I fell in love with Lucca back in 2017 when we visited the walled city for four days. Our criteria for the perfect Italian town have always remained: (1) beneficial location on a train line; (2) somewhat flat and *bicicletta,* bicycle-friendly; (3) ample shopping and restaurants nearby; and (4) it should have a friendly vibe. Bingo—Lucca satisfies all our criteria.

☙

Our new friends told us about a group of English speakers who meet every Monday at Bar del Sole for about two hours. "English Mondays" meets currently at the Mercato del Carmine right next to the bar from four o'clock until six o'clock in the evening. The Mercato had been known as the Convent of the Carmine in the 1930s. They turned this open area into a market with about thirty shops, but after years of neglect, it sits vacant. There are a few shops, including a favorite chocolate and coffee shop of ours along one perimeter. Rumors constantly run rampant about recovering the market for food shops and space for cultural and entertainment activities. Progress is slow, and I doubt it will come to fruition during my lifetime. You know how fast things take place here in Italy. Anyway, our weekly meetings occur in this beautiful empty space. It's a chance to chat and share information and stories with people from all over the world. Most ex-pats are from the States, but we've enjoyed meeting and becoming friends with people from Australia, Germany, Canada, France, and Brazil. We've learned some particularly important things just by attending this casual social event. We didn't realize so many ex-pats had claimed Lucca as home until our first time attending this group.

ଔ

There are two other valuable resources when it comes to living in Lucca. The first one is, *Tuscany's Grapevine Magazine,* a monthly publication that with keep you up to date on the events happening in and around Lucca, including oodles of other information.

The other great resource, LuccaNews.org, is an online website started by our friends, Diana and Sandy, who wanted to create a convenient place where expats could easily find information about living in Lucca. This site also includes upcoming events, articles, and a convenient bulletin board for messages. The Expats Menu is packed full of information about language schools, public transportation, and recommendations for things from veterinarians, translators, and other services.

ଔ

At this time, we also met new friends, Lita and Guy during an English Monday gathering. They live in France but also rent a beautiful, elegant apartment in Lucca. Lita is a fellow New Yorker, born and raised on Long Island. Yeah, you know we liked her right from the start. When describing them, they are complete opposites. Guy being a businessman is more reserved while Lita's presence alone can light up a room. They are both caring, kind, charismatic, and generous. Both are incredibly special and when in town, it is always a must to gather, socialize, catch up, and enjoy their company. They too are good friends with Gianna and Giacomo making gatherings extra fun.

During one visit to Lucca, Lita and Guy invited us over to their apartment for dinner with Gianna, Giacomo, and a mutual friend, Jean. Jean is French and lived in South Africa for several years. We enjoy listening when he shares stories of life in South Africa. He obviously speaks French but is also quite proficient in his Italian learning. He invests a good amount of time studying Italian, and it's quite evident when he speaks. Ilene is always a little jealous.

Enjoying a delicious dinner, the conversation lasted well into the late evening. We suddenly realized—it was well past curfew. Ilene rushed to help Lita clean up a bit, we thanked them for a wonderful evening, and headed down to the street. Jean took off on his bicycle while Gianna and Giacomo just live around the corner, so they didn't have far to travel.

Ilene and I said our goodbyes to them and headed down Via Fillungo. The streets were empty. There wasn't a creature stirring—not even a mouse. You understand the gist, and Ilene was concerned. She's wearing short boots and the noise of her footsteps on the cobblestones echoed off the small, empty streets. *Click, click, click* as she tried to walk on her tippy toes. She whispered to me that her calves were beginning to burn. I slowed my pace and turned to see why she was lagging.

Ilene whispered, "I don't want the police to find us out after curfew and my shoes are going to give away our location, the sounds amplifying off the narrow, tranquil street."

I laughed out loud, and Ilene hushed me. "Do you think the police are going to arrest two old grey-haired people for being out a little after curfew?"

Ilene gave me a dubious look. I offered her my arm and she hooked hers in mine. We strolled normally down to our piazza and apartment. As we entered our doorway, Ilene's face displayed a bit of a smirk. Being a rebel is a bit unfamiliar to her.

☙

The weather became a bit chilly, and on April 12, a big storm hit Lucca. Safely inside, we watched the sky slowly darken. In a flash, the winds kicked up blowing leaves and debris into a swirling motion. I was sure we'd lose power but never did. This storm; however, did produce snow—the four-letter word Ilene dislikes with a passion. It wasn't much but regardless… it yielded those frozen ice crystals referred to as snow. Social media became flooded with photos from residents showing off the streets and the Piazza dell'Anfiteatro dusted in white. Quite a beautiful sight, and certainly something we'd never experienced in Italy before. Three or four hours later the snow was gone. Only the memory and pictures of it lingered.

☙

Italian Ministry of Health:

On April 26, Tuscany will become a "yellow" zone

Again, new rules were posted by the Ministry of Health. It became grueling keeping up with all the changes. Most of Italy would become "yellow" zones and Tuscany showed signs of being among those regions. I couldn't wait to tell Ilene because our life in Lucca would change for the better. Restaurants, bars, and cafés would finally open with outside-only service starting that day. Little steps… but positive little steps. This news was great for us to hear, but we could only imagine how great it sounded to the residents of Lucca and Italy in 2020— locked down for over a year.

☙ Italy Begins to Reopen ❧
Ilene

We both decided it was time to look for ways to learn better Italian. Our friend, Barbara from Kentucky, gifted us her deposit at Lucca Italian School (LIS). She was scheduled to come to Lucca to take Italian lessons but when COVID hit, she prepared to evacuate, forced to return to the States. She contacted the school and they agreed to let us apply her deposit toward our lessons.

We began taking one-hour private lessons with a lovely young teacher, Ilaria. The school building is quite traditional looking, and the architecture is stunning. I imagine it existed as a villa at one time or another. It's something we looked forward to attending each week. We chose not to do group classes as they met every day, Monday through Friday, for four to five hours a day. As much as we want to continue to learn Italian, we are indeed "retired," and this rigorous schedule just didn't appeal to us. Perhaps taking an intense course for a few weeks would be all right with me, but I'm not sure I could convince Gary. He enjoys his free time and the slow-paced life we are experiencing in Italy.

On nice days during class, we'd sit out in the garden under the large trees for shade. Whiteboards on portable artist easel stands, along with table groupings scattered throughout the yard, served as outdoor classrooms. We enjoyed classes outside as it enabled us to not wear our masks.

It's difficult to learn a language from someone when you can't see their entire face—mainly their mouth and how they are pronouncing words. Masks muffle sounds and I found it difficult listening to our teacher while she wore hers. Pronunciation is a big part of the Italian language and one I struggle with, hence my added frustration.

Our one-hour class always flew by and Ilaria made learning quite fun. Studying grammar and verbs is brutal but she became creative, playing games she created to aid our learning process. She encouraged Gary and me to read aloud, alternating turns, to feel more comfortable speaking, not just learning.

☙

As a child, Gary grew up listening to his Italian grandparents on his father's side speak Italian. Perhaps I should clarify, as they didn't quite speak Italian—they spoke Sicilian, which is a whole different ballgame. They'd speak English to their grandchildren, but Sicilian to each other. In my perspective, at least Gary heard another language. He at least acquired a basis for learning Italian as a child. I, on the other hand, had no such experience. I never even took foreign language courses while attending high school. It wasn't a requirement, and my school day was comprised of all business-type classes such as typing and machine shorthand. *Certo,* of course, I regret it now. No matter what anyone says, I still feel it's harder to learn a language the older you become, especially after not hearing it spoken while growing up.

☙

When we told our grandchildren, they laughed at the thought their Nana and Jaja attended school. This is how our grandchildren identify both Gary and me. I wanted to use the term, "Nana," because my mother bore this nickname by her grandchildren. Gary's Polish grandfather who raised him was called Jaja, hence his use of the family tag. The thought occurred to me that perhaps the older grandchildren weren't really laughing at all, but completely horrified thinking school never ends if their grandparents are *still* attending.

☙

We instantly noticed during a walk on Friday, April 23, that things started changing. Change was evident, and the atmosphere was filled with activity, even a bit of frenzy. Restaurants were accepting daily food deliveries. Trish, a blog subscriber who lived in Lucca for a year, favored a restaurant called, "Blend" located in Piazza San Giusto. We stood and watched the activity… yes, something was different. At that moment it clicked. Umbrellas began to open, and tables and chairs, that were stacked, dirty, and bound together, were being cleaned and arranged. It became a beautiful day. We walked further down the main shopping street in Lucca, Via Fillungo. Strolling, we observed activity everywhere. I took out my list from Trish about other stores and restaurants she recommended.

"Let's check out a few of them and see if they show any signs of opening," I said to Gary.

As we found each recommendation by Trish and several Facebook followers, we made a mental note. Some of our faithful followers like Shari from Utah and Jackie from Indiana asked us to check on certain restaurants and *cafés* they've enjoyed on past trips to Lucca. They would like to know if they are still in business and open. We report back to each of them our findings. Some had good information to report, and other reposts—were not so good. It remained a tragedy some businesses just couldn't hold out for the tourists to return. We assume locals cooked at home more than they did before, probably to the dismay of many mammas.

ଓ

Gary and I had decided to celebrate Monday, the 26th with a live video on Facebook. To "go live" in a piazza on the first day restaurants could open with outdoor seating in over a year. I posted the announcement on our social media, Facebook and Instagram, denoting the day and time. Our Facebook page can be found by searching Our Italian Journey, and we are ItalianJourney on Instagram.

We headed to Piazza dell'Anfiteatro, our choice for our "live" event. It's a beautiful public square in the northeast quadrant of the walled center of Lucca. The ring of buildings surrounding the piazza follows the elliptical shape of the former second-century Roman amphitheater. Medieval houses rise three and four stories in a warm Tuscan palette of gold, cream, and various shades of light and dark ochre.

Laundry day is also quite obvious when strolling in this piazza. It adds to the charm. I often tease Gary… if someone hung a tiny, lacy pair of women's unmentionables here, photos would go viral in a matter of moments on social media. Although a more touristy area, there are quite a few restaurants within this charming piazza. Some are better than others. It is a great place to enjoy an Aperol Spritz, a hugely popular Italian *aperitivo,* and "people-watch." You can sit here for hours and just take in the atmosphere. It's entertaining to see where people congregate depending on the sun's location inside the piazza.

ꕤ

Choosing a restaurant, we sat at a table and, at four o'clock, I took out my phone. Our waiter Stefano arrived and took our order for two Aperol Spritz and two different types of bruschetta. Aperol Spritz is an Italian wine-based cocktail, commonly served as an *aperitivo.* It consists of Prosecco, Aperol, soda water, and a slice of orange. It has an unmistakable bright orange color. Invented by the Barbieri brothers in Padova in 1919, it's low in alcohol with a pleasant citrus, and bitter flavor. It has a light refreshing taste and is a favorite year-round. In Venice, however, these traditional drinks are served with a lemon instead of an orange—the reason is unknown to me. Just in case you're wondering, an *aperitivo,* or *aperitif* as the French call it, translates to the term meaning "to open" and refers to an alcoholic beverage that is meant to be consumed as an appetizer. It's the United States version of "happy hour."

ꕤ

We began the live feed with several people commenting right away. People from Peru, Arizona, Boston, Norway, Michigan, Australia, Canada, New Jersey, Florida, Ohio, Nebraska, Minnesota, Cartagena, and many other places attended our live broadcast. Gary and I were shocked at the interest. Even our waiter, Stefano, photo bombed and said hello. Twenty-two minutes later we signed off with comments still pouring in. It took me days to hopefully answer all the questions. When all was said and done, we wound up with over 250 shares, 375 comments, and 30,000 views. We knew people loved Italy—we just didn't realize a Facebook video of us sitting in a piazza could draw such interest.

After the live video ended, we wanted to see for ourselves if the restaurants were filled with residents longing for the day when they could finally enjoy an *aperitivo* outside. For the citizens of Lucca, they've waited over a year for true freedom. Not enough freedom to travel, but the simple pleasure of enjoying a meal or *aperitivo* outside with a few friends or family. Even pets likely experienced a bit of craziness during the lockdown. At that moment, things appeared to be getting back to normal—whatever that looks like now.

ɞ

Many friends told us that at the height of the pandemic, the Renaissance doors at several *portas* weren't technically closed, but you had to provide a pre-filled form anytime you left your house. You were only allowed to leave the historic center for specific purposes such as being an essential worker or an emergency trip to the hospital. Can you imagine the odd feeling the Lucca residents experienced being isolated inside the wall? To experience this isolation daily for an entire year? Outside-the-wall residents—foreigners, referred to in Italian as *stranieri*—were similarly affected. How did they feel not being able to enter the historic center? What a strange time for all of us. I'm sure each one of us has a story to relate to about this time in our lives.

ɞ

Italian Ministry of Health:

June 1: Restaurants, bars, and cafés will open with indoor seating

---

The Ministry of Health announced restaurants, bars, and *cafés* would open for service with indoor seating—properly spaced. Italy was also prepared to allow European Union tourists as of the first of June. The best news for us, possibly for USA visitors as well. Things were starting to look up, not just for us, but for Italy in general. Tiny steps, but important and exciting steps.

๛ *Estate,* Summer ๛
(June 21 - September 20)

ঌ The Choice: Lucca ৎ

Gary

Since we had decided to make Lucca our home, we needed to start the process of becoming residents. The first thing we needed to accomplish—finding a place to live. Should we buy or rent long-term? Did we want to live inside the wall or just slightly outside? After some discussion over a bottle of wine, our preferred method to obtain a conclusion, we ultimately arrived at our decision—to rent long-term, inside the wall. Time might change our decision but for now, it made sense. What did we want our Italian home to look like? After narrowing down our criteria, I began the search. Ideally, our apartment would include two bedrooms, two baths, an elevator, or just a few steps, and at the top of our list—outdoor space. Not a teeny, tiny balcony you can't even use, but decent space for at least a table and chairs. In addition, a small barbeque space would be over the top. I used three search sites, including Casa.it, Idealista.it and Immoblieri.it. Each of these sites hosted the same rental listings. The price and square footage varied slightly, but the photos were the same. We realized that working with a real estate office would be a wise thing to do.

At the next English Monday meeting, we asked several people in the group if they could recommend a realtor. Several members suggested one company, so we decided to contact them. The company, Vacation in Lucca is owned by two sisters, Rugiada, Margarita, and Margarita's husband Roberto. Margarita and Roberto agreed to meet with us and begin our search. Their main business was showcasing and selling high-end homes, but they had several beautiful vacation rentals available for us to see as well. With all our criteria and desires written down, we made an appointment with them to discuss what might be available in the Lucca market.

cs

Shopping for a home or apartment in Italy was completely different than back in the United States. What a real estate agent *thinks* you should have—is different than what *you think* you want. For example, if you recall, we wanted a furnished apartment with two bedrooms, two baths, and no higher than two floors up. At seventy-one years old, I don't want to scale Mount Kilimanjaro with two bags of groceries and six bottles of wine in my arms. Trust me, it's hard enough for me to climb steps let alone with groceries.

When in Arezzo during 2019, we walked approximately one mile to arrive at the grocery store, downhill—a piece of cake. Of course, it meant we experienced the reverse, suffering the same distance uphill with both hands full of groceries. On top of that, we had to scale two flights of steps to arrive at our apartment. There is no way I want to tackle it again.

Conversely, at least Lucca's Centro, or central area, is flat. We viewed several apartments with balconies so small you couldn't even display a flowerpot let alone a table and chairs. As I stated, we were being shown what they thought we would like—not necessarily what we requested to see. Finally, after seeing four or five apartments, the team started showing us apartments closer to what we wanted and of course, most, if not all, were out of our budget. I realize though, they were trying to grasp an idea of what style and certain look we were trying to find in our new home.

cs

After a few weeks of seeing apartments and making no progress, I decided to take matters into my own hands and start searching the Internet myself. I used the sites I mentioned to help in this quest. After six or seven hours of looking through hundreds of apartment listings, I settled on twenty or so I thought we should investigate. I sent the listings to our realtors and asked them to set up appointments for us to go see them.

After a few days, we received a phone call advising us that about two-thirds of the apartments were no longer available, and some were only holiday or short-term rentals. At this point, we settled on six apartments to explore.

The following day, we received a phone call from Margarita saying she'd set up three appointments for us to look at apartments. One had two bedrooms, two bathrooms, no terrace, and the kitchen existed in a narrow closet. While the apartment was in a nice area, not having a real kitchen was not ideal. We both love to cook and having a kitchen too small for both of us was a deal breaker. The next two apartments were situated on the other side of Lucca's historic center and in a quieter, more residential part of town. We chose to see the small apartment first—just a one bedroom and bathroom but featured a 340-square-foot terrace.

ᘓ

As we walked into the apartment, which was on the first floor and only seventeen steps, Ilene immediately turned to her right and entered the kitchen. I chose to go to the left into the living room followed by a jaunt to the terrace. I had a sneak peek at the apartment photos online, so I kind of knew what to expect. As Ilene stood in the kitchen in total bewilderment at the very basic furnishings, I called her to come into the living room. She very slowly walked up to me with this blank stare, shoulders slumped, and eyes rolling. I quickly placed my hands on both her shoulders, turning her slightly to face the terrace. She dashed through the door to the terrace, opened her arms wide with her palms facing up, taking it all in. She stood there with her mouth open in total disbelief at what could become our outdoor space.

Margarita caught Ilene's expression and asked her if she liked the terrace, and without hesitation, she replied, "Yes, I l-o-v-e it."

The living room was a decent size with only one IKEA couch, one old square French provincial-style coffee table, and a television with a modern corner stand. The room size had possibilities, with enough space to put in a few more furnishings to make it comfortable. Next, we walked into the bedroom. Once again, Ilene's jaw dropped in amazement. The room was furnished very nicely and featured a beautifully frescoed ceiling. It was detailed in gold, tan, burgundy, and blues with a medallion circle in the center. The extremely large border extended down at least eighteen to twenty inches from the ceiling onto the four walls. It resembles a fresco type of ceiling, but it might be considered decoratively painted—not technically a fresco.

We looked at each other and I said, "Imagine waking up to this every morning?"

Margarita inquired, "Are you ready to see the next apartment?"

She mentions this apartment hadn't been listed yet but would be within a short time.

"Should we put this on the potential list?" she continued.

After a moment, Margarita told us the rental price. Ilene shot me a quick look. A bullet couldn't have reached me faster. We asked for a moment alone to discuss it further and walked into the kitchen. After a brief discussion, we didn't even want to see the other apartment—we would take it. Even knowing the amount of work it needed, especially in the kitchen, the apartment included the all-important large terrace and a frescoed ceiling bedroom. What more could we ask for? With the low rental price, we wouldn't be house poor. It would leave us more funds to travel and dine out. We also didn't know at this point what utilities would cost. We had heard utilities were substantially higher in Italy than what we were used to in the United States, and we needed to allow for this expense. By the way… did I mention it's one flight up, seventeen very easy steps? Have our hearts found their home?

ᴄᴓ

Ilene

Maurizio and Patrizia are our wonderful landlords. They know we are learning Italian and encourage us all the time. We signed a "three plus two" lease meaning we can rent the apartment for three years, then if a family member doesn't need the apartment, we can stay another two years with no increase in rent. A common practice in Italy. There's also a "four plus four" lease plan representing the same concept except for a longer period. The amazing thing in Italy? The government watches out, so to speak, for the renter. Let's assume we decide we don't want to stay, our contract says we must give our landlord ninety days' written notice. Even though we signed a contract for five years, we could be released from the contract with this notice.

ᴄᴓ

Maurizio has a great presence about him. He's genuinely warm and kind, and in the next few visits, we become better acquainted. Mindful that we were working on learning the Italian language, one day Maurizio looked at me and presented me with a challenge.

He stated, "Come January, we only speak in Italian."

Swallowing a bit hard, I replied, "I hope to," not thinking a few months stood feasible but I didn't want to look like I wasn't trying.

Thank goodness for translating apps. I know they aren't always perfect, but I can act like I'm trying when texting him.

ᴄᴓ

While on this subject, many ask us about the logistics of travel in Italy and whether, when traveling, renting an apartment through a site such as Airbnb or a hotel is more suitable. When it comes to long-term rentals, meaning more than a month at one time, we've always found a site such as Airbnb better suited for our needs and budget. Hotels are more convenient when we are visiting a city for a few days. Although, I know some friends who only use sites such as VRBO or Airbnb. Are you aware you can negotiate the price on these sites too? We've made slightly lower, reasonable offers in the past enabling us to stay within our budget.

An important fact to keep in mind when mainly renting in a historic center—*any* historic city center—consider the location. Not so much where the apartment rentals are found, but from the standpoint of the trash receptacles. In the summer, walking past these can be brutal. What's more atrocious… if you have an apartment window near one of these receptacles, you'd never consider opening your windows to enjoy the fresh air. Then there is the physical part of the trash collection. The deafening sound of crashing glass, even for a brief moment, is enough to make you jump off the couch. We've been told depending on the type of trash container, it could be five to seven times a day the trash is collected. You grasp the picture—again, consider the location.

☙

Right now, the days are warm and long in Tuscany. First and foremost, on my list—cleaning. Italy's standards are completely the opposite of mine when it comes to cleanliness. I realize I'm a bit of a clean freak but the number of days it took to just clean the bathroom to my standards became ridiculous. Everyone has their quirks, and I have mine. Days of sitting in the shower, scraping and scrubbing, until all my nice, manicured nails vanished. It took weeks before we could finally arrive at a point to take a break. A much-needed break.

☙

We did encounter a hilarious moment when Gary and I were both meticulously scrubbing the kitchen. Every nook and cranny needed attention. The kitchen was scarce of furniture, but before we went shopping at IKEA to buy a pantry and cabinet for our dishes and glasses, we decided to get a bit more cleaning done.

It was a hot, humid day so along with all the windows open, we did the same to the front door. We figured it would let in even more of a breeze while on our hands and knees, and just might help cool us off. With the apartment windows open, the draft in this small entryway becomes a wind tunnel, and you must be careful. On a few occasions, the front door almost slammed shut while talking to someone in the lobby. You guessed it… I could've easily been locked out. I'm reminded of Marilyn Monroe in 1954 when she stood on a subway grate in New York City wearing a white dress fighting the upward breeze. Not thinking anything about it, we left our cellphones in the living room, as well as both our bags on the couch. What could go wrong?

We soon found out… with all the windows open, the wonderful breeze turned out to be a very big issue. Suddenly, the wind picked up and walloped the kitchen door shut with a deafening, *b-a-n-g!* When you walk into our apartment, on *destra,* to the right of the little foyer is the kitchen, where we were both cleaning. To the *sinistra,* on the left of the foyer, lies the rest of the apartment. With the layout clearly in your mind, perhaps you can gather our predicament. The door slammed so hard, that it broke the handle and we found ourselves stuck, stranded inside the kitchen. The noise alone scared the life out of me and when I jumped up, my eyes opened wide with the realization of the situation we were in… *Now, what do we do?*

I suffer from a little claustrophobia. Not bad—I just prefer window blinds open rather than closed but things like entering an elevator isn't an issue. Perhaps you can't even call it claustrophobia, but it's something along those lines and my heart started to beat faster as our predicament became apparent. Off my knees in a flash, I raised my shoulders and with open palms, gave Gary a terrifying look.

"How do we get out of here?" I stated a bit loudly and frantically.

Knowing how animated I am, I'll assume my arms were flailing a bit, too. Gary takes a moment to think.

On instinct, I went to the open windows and called out, "*Salve,* hello," hoping and praying one of our neighbors hears me.

Today, no response. Almost every other day, I can hear neighbors carrying on a conversation with their spouse, child, or hear others chatting on their cellphone—but not today. If we had crickets, they would be chirping.

I began walking around the table in the center of the room. After about three or four laps, Gary searches the empty drawers and discovers a knife.

Right away I ask, "Will it work?"

Now, I'm a wreck… and Gary? He's as cool as a cucumber. "Guess we'll see," he replied.

After a few minutes of using the knife as a screwdriver, he removes the locking mechanism and handles. Mission accomplished—we're free. As I regained my composure, I thanked Gary for thinking outside the box and finding another use for the knife. Without delay, Gary removed the door. The matching one, at one time on the other side of the foyer, had already been removed by the time we arrived at the apartment. The kitchen door joined the other one down in the basement storage area for the company.

୨ Tony, "The Guy" ୧

Gary

With apartment hunting completed, we set our sights on becoming residents and all it entailed. High on the list, transfer the utilities in our name and open a bank account to pay our rent. Italy does not allow the use of autopay using American credit cards—there went our mileage points. This checklist also included the task of obtaining our *Tessera Sanitaria* (Italian Health Insurance Card) for our medical coverage, which is free to all retired Italian citizens. Yes, you read correctly, f-r-e-e. Since we are retired and dual citizens, we qualified. With neither of us fluent in Italian we knew we would need help to accomplish all of this. Enter "Tony the Guy." I texted Tony using WhatsApp, discussed our situation, and asked for his help.

☙

Our residency cards were necessary to register our apartment lease with the city of Lucca. The card's also necessary to open a bank account and utilities transferred in your name. This became priority number one. Once you file for residency, the city has forty-five days to approve it. This necessitates a visit by the police to physically visit your *casa,* home to make sure you are living in Lucca. About two weeks after filing, we received a letter in the mail advising that we should expect a visit from a police officer—again, sometime in the next forty-five days.

Approximately two hours later the very same day, we heard a buzz from our doorbell. Our apartment features a video screen doorbell, as most do in Italy, but Ilene couldn't quite make out who stood at the building door. This happens quite often as people don't stand right directly in front of the camera and it's difficult to catch a glimpse of them. Normally, our routine is to open the door with a push of a button, then open our apartment door, and descend five steps to the landing by the staircase. From this perspective, we can see whom we've just allowed access to the building. Usually, it's a meter reader for the gas or electric or the *Poste Italiane,* post office.

Today's visitor turned out to be a policewoman. Upon entering the foyer, she stood next to all the bicycles neatly lined up in a row, paused and asked, *"Blessing?"* Dressed in the official dark navy-blue uniform with a white hat, she followed Ilene back to the apartment door after Ilene acknowledged with a simple, *"Si."* Ilene's maiden name is "Blessing," and one she must use in Italy. Ilene invited her in, but she stood at the bottom of our few steps and asked several questions. The officer asked her in Italian to confirm her name, birthdate, and place of birth. Since she heard me clanking some pots in the kitchen, she asked Ilene if I'm home as she needed me personally to answer the same questions. Ilene assumed this to be the gist of what the officer was asking. After confirming the information and answering her questions, she bid us *"Buongiorno"* and left.

I looked at Ilene and said, "Boy, I'm glad we received the letter today otherwise I would've wondered why a police officer stood at our door."

I presumed since the police visit occurred, everything else would just move smoothly along. How naive could I be? It's Italy, nothing is easy or on time. Why would this situation be transacted any differently?

☙

Several days after our police visit, Tony called and told us he made the appointment for us to physically obtain our residency cards. He told us we would need to bring two passport photos along with our passports. We found a little shop in town and acquired a photo package. It wasn't cheap but it's the only place we could find on short notice.

We met Tony in front of the commune and went inside. While Ilene and I sat waiting for our turn, Tony walked into one of the offices. When he emerged, he waved for us to follow him. As luck would have it, we weren't prepared. Somehow, we were still registered in AIRE, we needed to receive the paper version of the *Carta D'Identita*, not the easy plastic credit card type. The paper one entailed three passport pictures, not just the two we brought with us. Ilene was angry with herself because the photo package held more than just the two photos we brought. *Why would I bring more than we need?* she asked herself before we left for the appointment. Erring on the side of caution, we should've just brought the entire pack of photos. You know what they say about hindsight.

In a split second, Tony disappeared for a few moments, reappeared, and waved his arm in a fast motion to hurry and follow him. He took us to a photo machine just down the hall, like the ones you would take silly pictures in as a kid. We each took a turn taking new photos and went back to the office to finish our residency cards. With Tony's quick thinking, we didn't miss a beat with our appointments and sat right down to finish the applications. One process down, many yet to go. If you are wondering what AIRE stands for, it's the acronym for *Anagrafe degli Italiani Residenti all'Estero*, meaning a registry of Italians residing abroad. Registration is mandatory for all Italian citizens who transfer their residency abroad for at least twelve months.

ꟹ

The very next day I received another call from Tony telling us he made our appointment with the bank for our checking account. In a few days, we would need to bring our new residence cards, passports, and a copy of our official apartment rental agreement to the bank appointment. No problem I thought, we're prepared. We arrived at the bank at ten o'clock for our appointment and proceeded to the cubicle where our representative waited. A nicely dressed woman sat at her desk and we noticed right away she spoke very little English.

At once, Ilene leaned over to me and whispered, "Thank goodness Tony's with us." I agreed.

Everything ran smoothly until she asked for our phone number. You must possess an Italian phone number to open an Italian bank account. The number we're using would appear in the system as a third-party Italian number and the bank's computer wouldn't accept it. The first three numbers show whether a phone number represents a landline or a mobile number. Even though technically, our phone number is a mobile number, it didn't contain the correct three digits the computer system wanted and expected. No matter how hard she tried, the computer wouldn't accept our number. At one point she called over several other employees to see if they could bypass the system in another way. No such luck. So, after one hour and forty-five minutes and signing twenty or so documents, we would need to make another appointment once we obtained the Italian cellphone number to finish the process.

Now mind you, they never call you, and as a matter of fact, they only communicate through email or their phone app. Despite this fact, to keep everyone happy we opened an account with TIM, Italy's telecommunications company. Our next appointment went without a hitch, and we were now the proud owners of an Italian bank account. During this bank appointment, Tony gave us photocopies of our *Tessera Sanitaria* cards saying we should receive them in the next few days. We didn't go anywhere or do anything. Tony already did all the legwork. We engaged our realtors to help set up the utilities since they had a few connections and were knowledgeable. I would describe Italy's bureaucracy as a Catch-22. Even when you follow the rules, and do everything by the book, the rules can change often and without notice. Thank you, Tony, as you are truly "The Guy." Our guy.

❧ Le Mura ❧

Back in 2017, I instantly fell in love with this town for several reasons, but the main reason… *le mura,* the wall. It's the first thing you see as you near the historical area of Lucca. Whether you arrive by train as we did, by bus or car, it's there right in front of you. To enter the city center or historic center, you enter through one of the main *portas'* or gates as they are called here. They are Porta Elisa, Porta San Donato, Porta San Jacopo, Porta Santa Maria, Porta Victor Emanuele/Sant Ana, or Porta San Pietro. The wall encompasses the historic center and approximately 4.2 kilometers or 2.5 miles around the city. It's the only fully intact wall of its kind left in Italy today, and one of the most awe-inspiring sights I've seen in my life. I often find myself just gazing at *le mura* and wondering what life had been like living inside the wall while the neighboring cities tried to conquer Lucca.

❧

Lucca city center actually has three walls. The first wall had been constructed by the Romans and lasted until about 1000 A.D. There are still pieces of the wall visible to see. As Lucca grew, the second wall emerged. It's known as the medieval wall and parts of it still exist. The Anfiteatro or Roman amphitheater became incorporated into the medieval wall. The current wall, known as the Renaissance wall, was built in the sixteenth and seventeenth centuries. The purpose of this final wall was to encompass the expanded size of Lucca as a fortress. With invaders from Pisa and Florence, especially the Medici, trying to conquer Lucca, the new wall kept them out. In fact, Pisa failed many times as did the Medici family. The Medici tried several times to invade Lucca but were stopped every time they attacked. Frustrated that they could not conquer Lucca from the ground, they even elected a member of their family a Pope, trying to conquer Lucca through the church. Fortunately for Lucca, that attempt also failed. Lucca is one of the only cities in Tuscany that never fell under Medici rule. I imagine it's another one of the reasons why I love Lucca. You must respect a city standing up to the most powerful family in Tuscany and beating them mercilessly at their own game. As the Medici found out, there's more to *le mura* than meets the eye. *Le Mura* is built with bricks, and with tons of soil supporting this brick, made it impervious to cannon balls. A masterpiece of engineering for its day.

ଓ

One of the features many people are not even aware of are the passageways, tunnels, and barracks the troops used throughout the structure. For defensive purposes, Lucca could move men,

cannons, munitions, and food under the wall without being detected by invading forces. The cannon batteries were positioned to trap incoming forces in a crossfire. The lookout posts, along with the gun/bow stations, were all hidden from view. The enemy never saw troops moving above the wall because they used the tunnels instead. All the munitions, artillery, soldiers, and supplies were hidden from plain sight which made Lucca virtually impenetrable.

With the unification of Italy in 1860, the new Italian government decided the wall no longer served a purpose for defense. At first, they wanted the wall taken down, but they needed money to run the new country, so Italy decided to sell the wall back to Lucca and in 1870 the city of Lucca bought its wall back for the price of LIRA 112,350. With the advent of the euro in 1999, the wall cost Lucca approximately EUR 58,00. That's one heck of a deal.

Today, the wall is open for all people to enjoy, not just the Lucchese. We often take visitors through some of our favorite passageways under the wall. They are beautifully preserved and an architectural delight. One passageway has accented a column in slowly changing colored lights to showcase the framework. Everyone always marvels at these underpasses. On any given day you will see people walking, bicycle riding, doing yoga, sitting on the benches, or enjoying one of the four restaurants on the wall for a *caffè, aperitivo,* or a meal. For a history buff like me, it's a wonderful place to sit and imagine what life was like living here centuries ago. It's the perfect place to enjoy the sights and sounds of life in Lucca. The notion the Medici family never enjoyed life in this marvelous city makes me very happy. Although today, members of the Medici family can relish a visit to Lucca the same as you and me.

The Town
Ilene

Being in a flat, pedestrian-friendly town, we quickly decided to purchase bicycles. Everyone in Lucca has bicycles, even little ol' ladies and men. All are equipped with baskets in various sizes, on the front and even the back, and the all-important bell. The downside to Lucca, if there is one, is that bicycles are often stolen. Lucca is well known for its persistent bike thievery. We are not sure where they wind up, but even a heavy-duty lock doesn't stop the thieves if they want your *bicicletta.*

Gary and I considered buying two bicycles from a local shop in Porta Santa Maria. *Poli* is a name you will see on many of the bicycles around town. After visiting them one day, we found they only sported a few pink-colored used bicycles available for sale. I'm all right with a pink bicycle, but Gary is not willing to even consider riding through Lucca on a pink *bicicletta.* Even after informing Gary of my theory that the bikes would less likely be stolen due to their color, he still declined to buy a pink one. The higher cost of a used bicycle surprised me, so we decided we would wait and see what else we could find and pursue other options. Speaking of which, we always make sure to lock up the rear wheel to the bicycle frame, as it creates more difficulty for the thief. Why make it easier for them to snatch?

☙

Unbeknownst to me, there's a Facebook marketplace everywhere, not just in the States. *Who knew?* Upon researching, the used bicycles for sale appeared pretty beat up, and again, no great deals were available. Rather than paying such a high cost for a used bike, we should just invest in a new one with fewer problems.

So, we did. Using a cousin of a friend, we ordered two new bicycles equipped with six speeds, baskets, locks, and of course, bells, which are the most important accessory when riding the streets of Lucca. The sound of a bell means to "move over" or become run over by a passing resident on two wheels. We've heard it's illegal to ride your bicycle down Via Fillungo, the main shopping street in town. We've yet to find the signs and you'd never know with the number of riders down this relatively smooth cobblestone main street. On occasion, we've used Via Fillungo as a shortcut, but rarely, if ever, do we consider using this street on a weekend. The number of people walking this prominent street would make it counterproductive to try and travel anywhere fast.

Our friend, Giacomo texted us a photo of a "no bicycles" sign he spotted on Via Fillungo. During a recent conversation, I mentioned I've never noticed a sign even though I know you aren't supposed to ride on this busy street. Nonetheless, my question remained… *is it just a known fact?* The photo made me giggle. I knew the exact location where he took the photo, but the sign is so high up on the building—no wonder I never spotted it before. Since seeing the sign myself, I smile at it each time I bicycle past it. I'm such a rebel.

ꕤ

The absolute worst thing though, is when you spot a tourist taking a four- or six-seater rickshaw down this busy street. It's disastrous and causes major issues for delivery vans and pedestrians. The sad thing is they are usually told when renting these types of fun bicycles, not to go through the city center—to only use them on the wall. Not everyone follows directions. We've heard some horror stories.

Nevertheless, our bicycles take us almost everywhere. Back and forth to school, Brico, and grocery shopping at the large Esselunga. Brico is equivalent to a Home Depot in the States. Both are just outside the wall but an easy ride. The old and new hospital which we've already visited several times, again is an easy, convenient ride. We've become pros at knowing exactly how much and how heavy a load can safely be hauled home from a trip to the grocery store. Our three baskets and Gary's nylon saddle bags can hold quite a bit. We enjoy riding to the *Mercato,* as our teacher calls it, but it's more like a flea market that we all know and love. The most enjoyable thing to do on our bicycles, though, is riding *le mura*. Stopping and sitting with a *panini* for a picnic along one of the benches is the best way to enjoy lunch and a beautiful day.

ꕤ

Another amazing find in Lucca, other than Tony—is our handyman, Neil. Neil is a Scotsman living in Italy and has retained his beautiful Scottish accent. Neil, like Tony, can make things happen. The very first thing our new apartment needed was a barrier against those pesky *zanzara*, mosquitos who love me so very much. Too much. Without using any chemical plugins, I inevitably wake up with little bites on my face, looking like a young teenager with acne. Mosquitos love me, while for the most part, they leave Gary alone. However, the day I woke up with one on my nose, looking like Rudolph the red-nose reindeer, and one on my eyelid. *Basta*—enough.

"Call Neil," I bellowed to Gary from my position in front of the bathroom mirror.

Neil installed netting on all the windows and doors. They have a magnetic strip down the center enabling access to the shutters on the outside of the apartment. When the weather is bad or the sun too hot, you can close these slotted shutters while leaving your windows open for air. Most shutters in Italy are green in color—I've noticed other colors, but green is undoubtedly the most prominent color. The reason for this? In the past, it was believed painting shutters with arsenic, the green colorant for paint in the eighteenth-century, would help deter and kill insects—providing the windows even boast shutters, as some do not. Personally, I like the shutter look to a window and appreciate its function.

Neil solved a few minor issues in the apartment for us. He built a removable shelving unit for our huge middle closet in the bedroom, making it more usable for storage, as well as a pipe box in the *cucina,* kitchen to hide the ugly gas pipe in the corner of the walls. He also added a shelf over the washing machine, giving us more workspace. It aligned perfectly with the height of the stove and counter making it appear built-in. Job well done, Neil. *Perfetto!*

ᴥ

Although we did find one flaw in these mosquito screens. One day during the summer with our door open, Gary and I noticed a grey pigeon on the floor of our terrace. There's a story about this guy and his girlfriend, whom I call "Bianca." I realize these two lived here long before we arrived at the apartment, but let's face it, it's ours now—I declare it. Bianca is pure white and annoys me to no end. I can easily spot her sitting on a fence or tree in the backyard, especially on the wall surrounding our terrace. The prolonged cooing sound of a pigeon can wake me from a dead sleep. For me, it's like nails on a chalkboard—it's horrific. I despise the sound. So back to my story about Bianca's grey friend. He appeared hurt because even approaching him, he would hide behind a plant or the barbeque grill and not fly away. Still there she was, "Miss Bianca," sitting and watching us from the rooftop. She's indeed clever. Every time he would change his location on our terrace, so would Bianca. She's even bold enough to watch over him from the low wall of our terrace. Like clockwork, I would shoo her away.

On this day, Gary was sitting in his recliner in the living room while I was busy working on the computer in our bedroom. I rose from my chair and stood in the bedroom doorway in complete disbelief.

I said out loud, "Who invited you in here?"

Gary instantaneously jumped up from his recliner in bewilderment thinking I was talking to him. At the same time, who was walking through and under the netting? Bianca's grey friend, like he belonged in the apartment. It took Gary and me some strategic moves scurrying around the room to finally catch him and put him back outside where he belonged. We're not quite sure what happened to her grey beau.

Friends even bought us a water pistol to help chase Bianca away when she would land on the wall of our terrace. It would send her flying but she always returned. Even the plastic owl the landlord left didn't detract her from landing and enjoying our terrace. Nor did the sounds of prey I tried playing from my cellphone for hours on end.

☙

I became determined that Bianca would not beat me. The water pistol wasn't powerful enough to reach her when she'd land on the terrazzo wall. I was committed to showing her who was boss and deterring her from visiting us again. I turned on the water at the outdoor spigot, and with the spray nozzle set to the stream setting on the hose, I sat on the terrazzo. After thirty minutes of waiting for her to return—I gave up. Defeated, I looked up and around in the sky finding her nowhere in sight. Chalk up a win for Bianca. Later, white feathers and poop showed she'd returned when I wasn't around to confront her. She's winning this battle. I might need to just concede this fact.

℘ Summer Excursions ℘

Gianna asked me to go with her on a trip to Massarosa, which is in the province of Lucca. A few days earlier, she went with her husband, and found amazing flower fields and wanted to return to capture even more photos. I quickly consented as her sidekick and off we went. This oasis of beauty remains family owned and run, and this marshland had been originally classified as a rice field until the 1950s. Today it's filled with lotus flowers. You can take a bicycle, but we walked along the lotus flower trail. The elevated flat path is about one mile in length and connects the two towns of Bozzano and Massarosa.

☙

It's near the Bozzano train station, where we found and took hundreds of photos of the largest lotus flower cultivation in Italy. It encompasses about seventeen acres or seven hectares. The gates were locked, so we took our photos between the square metal openings. I was blown away by the various shades of white and pink all while listening to the birds singing their songs. The flowers looked so delicate and the extremely large, almost round leaves in various shades of green made a beautiful contrast. Of course, the younger leaves appeared a distinctively brighter green and still slightly curled at their tips. It equaled nothing I'd experienced before. Further down from this location are fields of sunflowers, lavender, eucalyptus, saffron, hops, and hemp. We never did find the lavender fields as Gianna's GPS took us down some pretty tiny roads, which might have been someone's driveway. We were so close, yet so far away. Perhaps next season we will try again to find the lavender field she enjoyed and found just a few days before with Giacomo.

℘ Andrea Bocelli ℘

My favorite Italian tenor is Andrea Bocelli. We've been fortunate to see several of his concerts in Arizona, but my heart has always wanted to see him perform in his hometown of Lajatico in Tuscany. The Teatro del Silenzio is an open-air amphitheater built utilizing the natural formations of the landscape. In 2006, Bocelli convinced his town to build this venue.

For my birthday, Gary booked an evening under the stars at the *teatro*. Reserved through a wonderful tour company, 2Italia, we were transported to the venue in a private vehicle and given a picnic basket filled with prosecco, wine, water, focaccia, dolce, and all sorts of goodies. Complete with plates, utensils, and a blanket in case the evening became chilly. The performance and stage lighting were spectacular, and the entire event was phenomenal. I'd seen photographs of this venue, but as with most photographs, they don't do the countryside justice. It was more beautiful than I could have imagined. Because of the pandemic, limited seating and spacing between chairs was quite evident. Our seats were in the middle section and just about dead center. The second-row seats on one of the tiered grass sections made our views unobstructed, and just incredible. I will never forget that event.

The music touched my soul. Music is a sound of love and a language that brings us all together. Under the incredibly beautiful setting, I'm emotional. I remember reading Andrea refuses to be defined by his blindness. He sees all the beauty and suffering in the world—but in a very different way, through his voice. For me, it became especially true that evening.

We gazed up at the town of Volterra sitting on one of the nearby hilltops. A warm glow from barely visible streetlights is clear. The moon was reflecting brightly over the Tuscan landscape illuminating the tall, thin Italian cypress trees lining a dirt road I'd noticed off in the distance. I love these trees and how they sway in the wind. The food tasted delicious and sitting next to the love of my life—priceless. Twenty years have passed since McCann-Erickson created the very first commercial for MasterCard's long-running "priceless" campaign. Good thing royalties aren't required as I use the phrase quite often.

ଔ

So, what is it about those trees, the symbol of Tuscany, that intrigue us all? They say the cypress tree stands between different worlds. Figuratively and literally, their tips point up toward immortality and hope. Our friend Diana told us an amazing story on a recent trip to Montecarlo—it captivated me. She told us about Cyparissus. In Greek mythology, Apollo beloved a boy named, Cyparissus. The favorite companion of this boy, was a tamed stag that he accidentally killed with his hunting javelin as it lay sleeping in the woods. The boy's grief became so extreme it transformed him into a cypress tree, a classical symbol of mourning. The shape of the tree resembles praying hands. I love seeing these trees along the hilltops driving through Italy, especially in Tuscany.

Norcia

Our landlord informed us about an event occurring each year in Italy. Something special, but only for a very limited time during the season. He texted me a link and when I looked at the photographs of the astonishing sea of color in this valley in Umbria, I instantly wanted to go. I sent Gianna the link as she's a talented photographer. As you may recall, birds are her obsession, but these flower photos might be something she'd enjoy photographing. The dazzling photos captured patches of vivid reds, bright sun yellows, and purples in various shades. Each photo was more breathtaking than the last. I knew she'd want to go as much as I did. We made plans to go to Castelluccio di Norcia and spend the night in the nearby town of Norcia. Their car makes these trips possible for Gary and me.

A few days after my birthday, and the Bocelli concert, we packed for our overnight trip to Norcia, stopping for lunch in Montefalco. Oh, this sweet little town is charming, as are most in Italy. Although similar, they each contain something special, individually setting them apart from other small towns. This town, in the region of Umbria, has been settled since pre-Roman times and retains many of its historic buildings. It's also well-known for its wine, Sagrantino. This wine is made with one hundred percent Sagrantino grapes and is one of the healthiest wines you can drink. It's high in antioxidants and boasts a deep, rich, dark purple color.

After walking the town, we enjoyed a bottle with a quick lunch. During lunch, we told the story of Gary enjoying gnocchi, a varied family of dumplings in Italian cuisine, cooked in Sagrantino wine when we stayed in Foligno. I vividly recall the evening when the waiter brought Gary a purple bowl of deliciousness. The little pillows of white gnocchi happily swam in their purple pool of wine. Gary informed our friends it was "divine."

☙

Approaching the town of Norcia, we instantly noticed scaffolding along the outside of the wall surrounding the historic center. The hotel in which we'd planned to stay overnight was inside the wall. This town has a special place in our hearts.

In 2016, while staying ninety days in Parma, we woke up one morning to several texts and emails from our family and friends back in the States. They all wanted to know if we were all right. Gary and I weren't sure what the fuss was about—until we turned on the television. Within a short period of time, a series of three earthquakes hit three towns in Umbria—Norcia being one of them. The strongest magnitude was 6.6, with the others just slightly less. We watched it unfold in front of our eyes. From August 24 to August 28, the town of Norcia and the surrounding area suffered no less than ten quakes and tremors, the devastation massive. While we informed everyone back in the States that we were physically fine, as the quakes were located far south of us, our hearts ached for what appeared on the news. The death toll rose as our hearts sank.

☙

While visiting Siena in 2017, we noticed an exhibit about Norcia. Curiously, we walked over to the sign and realized Siena is the "sister town" to Norcia. The exhibit temporarily displayed precious artifacts recovered from the earthquake until the church and town could be reconstructed. Several items caught our eye: five extremely large candlesticks on display survived the quake. These were from the front altar of Norcia's *duomo* with only one missing from the original group. The wooden cross looked like it was beyond repair, but who knows? We'd hoped that some artisan would be able to restore the cross to its prior beauty. Norcia became special to us, and we remain connected to this small town in some small way.

ঙ

After checking into our hotel, the attendant showed us some of the damage. Fortunately, they survived most of the major devastation with only a few minor issues in the main lobby of the hotel. Several rooms were completely closed until they could complete renovations.

Still early in the day, the four of us decided to drive to the location of the flowers. As Giacomo navigated the winding road, the views were spectacular. Castelluccio is a small village in Umbria found in the Apennine Mountains of central Italy. As we approached the top of the last mountain and began our descent to the valley below, I found myself holding my breath—waiting. Anticipating the beauty. We knew from the photos on the website exactly what to expect.

Suddenly, I heard Gianna say, "Oh no," from her location in the front passenger seat and I promptly sat up, poking my head between the front seats from the back seat.

I chimed in, "This can't be it." At the same time in my gut—I knew it was. The car remained silent… you could've heard a pin drop.

Were we too late? Did the height of the color bloom a week or two before? We spotted a few patches and rows of red poppies and some lavender down in the field. Giacomo pulled off the road for us to investigate. My heart sank and I think Gianna's did too. We both wanted to do blog posts and take hundreds of photos of our own. Spectacular photos like those from the website. As we all exited the car and walked through the fields Gianna made a great suggestion to head back to town and come back in the morning when it's cooler. The heat of the afternoon has closed most of the flowers. Being a good photographer, she knew this, and the decision became unanimous with fingers crossed for the morning.

ଔ

Back in Norcia, we began exploring. Scaffolding was everywhere. As we approached the main piazza, San Benedetto, we could see the clock tower standing proudly, already undertaking its restoration. As I stood looking at the *duomo* with only part of the front and back façade still standing, the entire center of the church—was gone—destroyed. The pile of rubble remained evident. Tears came easily to me as I recalled seeing the devastation unfold in front of our eyes while in Parma in 2016. It still stood exactly as it did in the photos we saw and in the videos on television. My emotions overwhelmed me—for a town I've never traveled to previously, I cried. I cried for the people of the town and for the people who died. Five years later, they are still rebuilding, still holding strong. It's difficult to see and witness the destruction up close.

We took our time, paid our respects, and walked the streets. Some streets were blocked off with tall, folding construction metal gates and notices written in Italian, of course. We assumed the streets unsafe, even now after all these years. I stood there, both hands gripped on the metal square fence just thinking about what happened. What if I lived down this street and wasn't allowed to access my home? We continued in silence, meandering and taking it all in, following one another. We were all struck by how resilient the residents of Norcia are. First the earthquake—then COVID. Wow.

Arriving in the main piazza, we noticed about fifty to seventy-five plastic school chairs along with a jumbotron. The Euro Cup was in full swing, and the townspeople were enjoying the event, together in the main piazza. After dinner, we joined the residents of Norcia and watched the UEFA Euro 2020 match between England and Denmark under the stars. On occasion I'd glance over at the *duomo*, standing quietly in the dark with rubble surrounding it. I closed my eyes… imagining what the town encountered standing here five years ago with the city crumbling all around, feeling what I imagined they must have felt… being surrounded by uncertainty as to what was happening. Emotions must have paralyzed some, panic-stricken and crying out to find family members. It's surreal to stand in a place of utter destruction and be able to feel the emotions that once filled the space.

ᴕ

Before we left Norcia, we stopped in one of the little shops. I collect dish towels from cities in Italy to use when making bread and pasta. The proprietor asked us in Italian where we were from. He was an ordinary looking older Italian store owner. I assumed this town wasn't receiving as many visitors as it did years ago.

At the same time, both Gianna and I replied, "Lucca."

The owner from behind the counter gave us an inquisitive look, slightly raising his shoulders. *Is it possible he didn't hear or understand us?* We gave each other a glance. We thought we would elaborate to help him understand.

Again, almost simultaneously we said, "… As in Tuscany?"

The humor of the moment then came to light. From the glint in his eye, we realized that we were both mispronouncing the name of our town... an "aha moment" for sure.

He then corrected us, saying "Luk-ka," with a strong accent on the second "c."

We all enjoyed a good laugh as apparently the way Gianna and I had pronounced it, we were actually referencing a man's name—not the city. From that day forward, we learned to pronounce the last syllable. Neither one of us heard the difference until then. Now when I say, "Lucca," I remember the old gentleman, making sure I pronounce the second "c" correctly.

Viareggio

Day trips exploring nearby towns became a weekly event. The train to Viareggio from Lucca is a comfortable twenty-minute excursion. Viareggio is renowned around the world for its shipbuilding and fishing industry as it is well situated on the Tyrrhenian Sea. Walking on the wide cement promenade with *cafés* and restaurants along its perimeter creates a pleasant experience, especially on a sunny day.

Toward the marina, you usually can find fisherman selling their catch of the day right off the dock. The long pier is another delightful walking experience just watching the small waves reach the long shoreline. To enjoy one of the most breathtaking views in Viareggio, you must continue further on this pier. You can catch a glimpse from walking on the beach but it's looking back in the direction of the shoreline when you notice the snow on the Apuan Alps. Although… it isn't snow you see. It might come off white but it's the quarries of the famous Carrara Mountains. This white treasure was popular with Michelangelo and Canova. Today, the Province of Massa-Carrara still appreciates the abundance of this beautiful marble.

☙

Also found on this long pier, is a bronze sculpture called, *L'attesa,* "The Waiting." The statue represents a family of a seafarer anxiously awaiting his return. It is said the statue stands for, "hope." It was made a permanent fixture in this harbor in 2007.

☙

This small seaside resort also possesses another beauty, a bit more subtle and perhaps you might not notice it at first. It's the beautiful architecture that began in the 1900s. Liberty style defines Viareggio's identity, and its connection to nature. This artistic culture, along with the beautiful soft-colored buildings, sets Viareggio apart from most other towns. On the Viale Margherita seafront, you'll still find one of Puccini's favorite hangouts. Its glittering Oriental domes are unmistakable at the Art Nouveau Gran Caffe Margherita. I understand their coffee is still pretty darn good, too. We often just take a train ride to walk the streets and admire the architectural style.

The seafood here is abundant as you might guess. There's no shortage of places to enjoy various kinds of gifts from the sea. We've often enjoyed stopping for a fritto misto along the long promenade but recently found a very nice sit-down white tablecloth type of place on the other side of the canal. Large boats turned into food trucks are often found docked by the main canal on the pier. The aroma when you pass—is heavenly… especially if you like seafood.

A stroll along Viareggio's promenade, commonly known as the "Passeggiata di Viareggio," sets the tone for this town. This seafront stroll is a great way to enjoy this beach resort. The promenade consists of a wide, flat, cement pathway running parallel to the sea. Along the side of the sea, you'll find bathing establishments or beach clubs bustling in the summertime. This area is not a public beach, and although you can walk along the shoreline, you'll notice in the summer, that the individual clubs, with their specific color and pattern or thatched umbrellas and lounge chairs, are all well staged and perfectly aligned in rows. It's fun to walk on the promenade and take note of all the different names of these private clubs. We've even found one called, "Arizona."

On the same side of the promenade but in front of the smooth sandy beach are the *cafés* and shops. The shops are filled with beautiful beach attire along this pedestrian walkway. We often just window shop and settle for gelato, even in the wintertime.

ঌ Florence ৲

Since arriving in Lucca, we've made several trips to our beloved town, *Firenze,* Florence. In fact, for both Gary and me, Lucca is similar to Florence—just on a smaller scale. This is, perhaps, the reason Lucca stole our hearts. We both connect with Florence, even though it's too large a city for us to consider calling it "home." Florence is an hour-and-a-half train ride from Lucca, and it makes for a very easy day trip. When needing to shop for clothing, even though Lucca has some wonderful small shops, we tend to visit Florence for this reason. We enjoy shopping at a few favorite shoe stores and leather shops here. We wouldn't consider purchasing these items anywhere else. Although a few of our friends mentioned a place in Lucca that makes personal custom-fit shoes which might be a consideration in the future.

Florence is just Florence. Spectacular in every way. When someone contacts us about planning a trip to Italy, my first question is always: "Have you visited Florence?" It's the perfect start to any trip to Italy. From Florence, you can easily travel to most other cities.

We always enjoy walking our favorite streets, window shopping, sitting in our favorite piazzas with gelato, and watching the hustle and bustle of this amazing city. A few places are always on the top of our list to see no matter how many times we go. We always must walk past the *duomo.* We enter now and again, but it's a sight to behold and always generates smiles on both our faces.

Walking through the Uffizi piazza or corridor is captivating, but exceptional when artists are set around the perimeter with their easels filled with their paintings and drawings. Most of the art pieces are landscapes, and mainly about Florence and Tuscany—images they'd captured on any given day sitting on a street or reminiscing about a trip taken recently.

From this location, the path always takes us through the arches of the Uffizi to the Arno River and the Ponte Vecchio Bridge. I could stand for hours watching the activity along the Arno. Long hull, narrow and sleek silhouette kayaks glide over the water with ease. The passengers make it look effortless, but I know better. It takes great strength to row a kayak. It's peaceful watching them.

Slowly they disappear under the glorious Old Bridge, and out of sight.

At sunset, the best view in the town is up at Piazza Michelangelo but again, not something we do each visit. It's quite a hike up the hill and we finally used the autobus once when we thought we just couldn't make the trek.

Our love of Florence will never die. I always wonder if we didn't choose Lucca, would it—could it have become our perfect Italian town? Even with the crowds? We loved our ninety-day stay back in 2017. Perhaps one day we just might find out. *Who knows?*

Borgo a Mozzano

We've visited the small town of Borgo a Mozzano several times, located an easy twenty- minutes by train from Lucca. This town is very long and narrow, built alongside the Serchio River. This charming town also has one of my favorite things to photograph. The Devil's Bridge with its asymmetric arches is also known as Maddalena's Bridge. It's an easy walk to the bridge, located at the far end of town.

There are several legends associated with the building of this bridge. One of the most popular proclaims that a master mason began its creation but soon realized he would not complete the work on the agreed day. Frightened by the consequences, he asked the Devil for help. The Devil accepted the task of completing the bridge in one night for a price. The cost… he would take the spirit of the first who would cross it. The contract was signed but the mason chose a dog to cross the bridge first, fooling the Devil and he became defeated. Of course, there are other versions of this legend, and you can choose to believe them or not.

On the other hand, the bridge remains a sight to behold, especially with the reflection of its arches in the water of the Serchio River. It's only for pedestrians and quite picturesque. During our first visit to the town, we noticed some type of construction work on the river upstream which enabled only a small trickle of water to pass under the bridge. This hindered my photography for the day as I couldn't achieve the sensational full-circle photo. This circle occurs with the reflection of the high arch of the bridge in the water.

A second trip turned out more successful, but I've yet to achieve the pristine photo I'm searching for. Perhaps I need to wait to retrieve my Nikon D3300 from the States and return to try again.

⸙ Adventure Meeting People ⸙

September became a very special month for us. People contacted us left and right about visiting Italy, Lucca in particular. My email became jammed with questions, asking for recommendations about Tuscany. It began with our good friend Bernie and her daughter, Laura. I'm not quite sure how Bernie and I became friends but I'm going to guess it developed after she found our blog. I hope my guess is correct. We've Zoomed with Bernie many times and enjoy the friendship we've made with her and her husband, Chip. This trip to Italy took them to quite a few towns and cities. I enjoyed watching her post photos on social media in some of our favorite places. Subsequently, Bernie contacted us and said she and Laura decided to visit Lucca for the day… to see us. We were thrilled, to say the least. Our first visitors to our new town.

Meeting them at the train station, we were all smiles. Stopping first for *caffè,* we sat and caught up on life—life for them in the States, and for us here in Italy. Bernie even surprised us with a gift bag filled with treasures from the States. Small items she thought we'd enjoy such as lotions, flavored water packets, several cute material masks, and two red, white, and blue dish towels. It was such a cute surprise. Once they caught their breaths, we showed them the highlights of our town and our little apartment.

We knew people expressed curiosity about what a true rustic Italian apartment looked like; we just didn't know how much until we did a live event. The number of people who tuned in for the event was staggering. The video started on our street, through the lobby to our apartment, taking viewers through each room, and ended on the beautiful terrace. Nothing more, just a quick tour. Yet it took us days to answer all the questions and comments resulting from the event.

After knowing Bernie for so long, it was so nice to finally meet her in person. Her lovely daughter too. The day passed so quickly—too quickly. We hope they both enjoyed their time in Lucca, seeing it through our eyes.

ଓଃ

We've spoken before about a great group, "mi.o" (Modern Italian Network) out of Baltimore, Maryland. This group offers so much diversity for those loving anything Italian. The language classes, educational information, and friendships we've enjoyed and shared warm my heart. Administrators, Gina and Matteo, do a sensational job managing a website for everyone to enjoy.

One such friendship generated through mi.o is with Peggy and Frank. They live in Baltimore but also rent a home in Narni, which is Frank's ancestral hometown in Umbria. After years of knowing them, and both now in Narni, we suggest using this opportunity to meet in person. Peggy and I are in the same Saturday language class and probably at the same level, struggling at times together. We decided to meet halfway in Grosseto, between Narni and Lucca. None of us had visited the town before so it would make a perfect adventure—exploring the town together and finding out a little more about each other and their lives in Baltimore.

Train schedules coordinated, we met for a few hours to enjoy each other's company. It's one thing to enjoy a friendship by email or even Zoom—but meeting an "Internet" friend for the first time, someone you already kind of know? A real treasure. Although we were able to investigate the town together, time didn't allow us to explore or enter any of the buildings, but of course, there's always time for lunch.

We parted ways at the train station, and because of unknown delays, it took us both forever to reach home. Occasionally, you must expect this with train travel. So many things affect the trains. Not sure we ever found out the cause of the specific issue that day, but I don't recall it being a strike. Strikes are typically announced ahead of time to limit the inconvenience to travelers. It's usually the employees taking a stand against the company. It's most often the local train lines and when it does occur, you just try and remain flexible. After all, you're in Italy.

ଓଃ

Meeting other friends, Dawn and Bob, was another sensational day. Dawn's another member of Mio, a talented author, and a great friend. We have many special memories of meeting people we know through social media or other groups, as well as friendships initiated in the States that blossomed during our travels through the common love of Italy. By the time Dawn and Bob came, Gary and I created a well-thought-out, choreographed walking route we would take to encompass all the major sites in Lucca. We're becoming tour guides, and we love it. We even started including a bit of history. One of Gary's favorite stories about Lucca—the Medici never conquered it, although they tried several times. Gary has read extensively on the history of Tuscany, and the Medici is not one of his favorite families from the Renaissance. Connecting with Dawn and Bob will remain a treasured moment. A moment in time we always will remember.

We've several favorite spots to show our out-of-town visitors. This planned walking route includes a fascinating exploration under the wall of Lucca. There are several passageways throughout the city, but we really enjoy the architecture of the one near our apartment.

☙

The other must-see—my favorite street in Lucca. Well, other than our street of course. If you walk down Via Fillungo too fast, you just might miss it. Near Torre delle Ore, the clock tower, you will find the narrowest of streets, Chiasso Barletti. The shop owners found on this street create a special atmosphere with various changing decors. Sometimes you'll find an actual red carpet, while other times you can find colorful wooden houses and flowers strung from side to side across the walkway. These decorations span the entire length of the small street. No cars could fit here but occasionally I do spot a Vespa, and always a few bicycles. During the Christmas holiday, the lights were especially enchanting on this street. Given that… there's also something very special about Chiasso Barletti street.

You can find Ettas'—a small English bookshop on this appealing little street. The owner's name is Julia, and her shop is named after her cat, Etta. Julia is lovely and speaks English. She carries hundreds of books… including ours. When we first arrived in Lucca, many locals said we must visit her. She instantly wanted to carry a few copies of our book, *Our Italian Journey,* and asked us to sign them for her customers. Two other authors live in Lucca and Julia carries their books too. We're thrilled and honored.

When visiting her store or just walking by, we always wave. She's so friendly and lets us know when her supply has run dry. She mentioned to us one day that several people have stopped in her store after meeting us. A few even bought a copy of our book.

☙

Another awesome visit we treasure came from executive chef and farmer friend, Margie from Little Rock, Arkansas. Another friendship originating from mi.o has blossomed into a whole lot more. We would take our Saturday language class together and Zoom separately once or twice a week to work on the lesson together.

Margie happened to be in Sicily filming a documentary for almost a month. It produced an awesome adventure following her through small farms, discovering food and families on this beautiful island. A means to become the sole of the soil. Margie insisted, that she couldn't be so close—just around the peninsula in Italy without coming for a visit. Sure enough, she came to Lucca for several days.

We visited our favorite hangouts, introduced her to our English Monday group, and Margie treated us to a day at a winery up in the hills of Lucca. Physically meeting her, enjoying good food, wine, and great conversation, enhanced our long-distance friendship. She has won awards for her one-acre sustainable farm specializing in seed-to-plate living. Originally a junkyard, Margie and her significant Chris, have transformed the property into something spectacular. She also offers amazing cooking classes with recipes from her Italian roots. We know she's close to publishing her first cookbook that will turn into a must purchase, and a gem for us.

☙

Also, during this time, two friends from 2019 re-entered our lives in Lucca, Nanette, and her son Joel from Florida. We met Nanette one night in Rome when Gary and I attended the opera,

Rigoletto by Giuseppe Verdi. A chance meeting in a balcony of a sold-out performance at the Teatro dell'Opera di Roma. Nanette overheard Gary and me speaking, and turned around to greet us. I recall telling her about our dual citizenship adventure and she informed us her family was in the same process with the Italian Consulate in Miami. I distinctly recall Gary taking out his Italian passport, again the elusive, maroon-colored book, and Nanette wanting to hold it in her hands. We parted ways after the amazing performance, agreeing to stay in touch. A few months later, when Gary and I stayed in Conversano in the Puglia region, we met Nanette again with her son, Joel. It turns out they're back in Italy, all these years later, and in Lucca. We needed to reunite.

Finding their Airbnb, we hugged as old friends, and we welcomed them both to Lucca. It's great to see them again and we quickly caught up with life's events. Nanette stayed for two weeks before continuing her journey through Italy, but Joel decided to make Lucca his home. Joel and his father were successful with their dual citizenship quest, while Nanette still waits for her confirmation.

In the next several weeks we helped Joel find an apartment and settle in. Our friends helped too, especially Betta, and we enjoy including Joel in our excursions around Lucca and holiday gatherings. He's a wonderful addition to the ex-pat Lucca community.

Betta is a treasure we met in Lucca through English Monday. She's beautiful in every way, inside and out. She's fierce in her determination to learn the Italian language and enjoy life in Italy. Unfortunately, for now, she also lives in San Francisco and travels between the States and Lucca throughout the year. When in town, she's a complete pleasure to be with and we love getting together. Her long light brown curls cascade over her thin body. I'm not sure where she puts her gelato, but it doesn't wind up in the same place mine does.

☙

Meeting people who've read our first book or subscribed to our blog has remained an unexpected pleasure in our lives. Several in our English Monday group continue to tease us we are attracting so many people to Lucca. They enjoy meeting all our new friends when we bring them to a Monday meeting. Our love for this town must shine in all we do. Life happens in Lucca—we are grateful for it every day. The adventure of meeting people and sharing our passion for Italy has brought us some of our most endearing moments. Never in our wildest dreams did we ever think people would want to meet us—just from reading our book. Or, just from finding our blog and enjoying it. We are humbled and appreciative. These experiences greatly enrich our lives, and we hope they continue.

ↂ

A perfect example of this type of friendship is with Paul. Paul and his family are also from Phoenix but own a second home in Volterra. This incredible hilltown is about seventy-two kilometers or forty-five miles south of Lucca. Quite a while ago, I received an email from Paul telling me he was currently reading our book while on an airplane with his wife. He told me he was enjoying reading the book. I responded right away acknowledging we appreciated it so much and would he mind his wife taking a photo of him with the book. He instantly emailed back, he didn't enjoy photos taken of himself *(who does?)* but would do it for us. Paul and I correspond often on social media and he's one of our loyal followers. He also mentioned he happened to be reading the section in our book where I mentioned wanting to experience bringing in the harvest for olives and grapes. He had an idea.

Their home in Volterra is set in an olive grove and they invited us to come harvest the olive trees when the time arose. Gary and I were excited but later learned that, unfortunately, this year wasn't possible. The extreme heat and drought in Italy caused the olive trees on their property to produce smaller and fewer olives. With olives not possible this year, Paul had another idea. Their friends owned a winery close by—one of those treasured connections—and he'd make the introductions.

ↂ

It's at the end of summer, marking the beginning of the grape harvest. It's an amazing time of year in Italy. Countless festivals are dedicated to wine and are held throughout Tuscany. When it comes to wine, we learned that most wineries have restrictions on who can assist with their harvest. It's a highly regulated industry, as you might guess. Assisting might not pan out unless we go to work on a farm, called an *Agriturismo* in Italy. An Agriturismo is almost always found in the countryside of any given region in Italy and it's a place to stay overnight and help with the farm and land. This might just materialize into an adventure for next year.

☙

Meanwhile, Paul connected us with Eva and Leonardo from Beconcini Winery. A very special place with a very special wine. Beconcini Winery is set in the Tuscan hills of San Miniato. They grow several types of Tuscan grapes but one, in particular, is a Spanish grape. After purchasing the property, they became versed in their land. DNA analysis proved some of the unknown vines were Tempranillo. These grapes are important for Spanish winemakers as it creates an integral part of Spain's most popular blends. The original pre-phylloxera grape in Tuscany, they guess, came to Italy around the nineteenth-century. Those passing through the original ancient Francigena pilgrimage route through their vineyard either dropped or left them. So, why am I talking about a Spanish grape in Italy? Because it's amazing.

After connecting with Eva by email and texts, she invited Gary and me as guests and friends of Paul to the Tempranillo di Toscana Wine Festa 2021 held on the first weekend in September. How could we refuse? Drinking wine in a vineyard amongst these beautiful grapes and dinner too? The anticipation and excitement started to build.

The first thing Gary and I thought of—our friends Gianna and Giacomo—as they also love wine as we do, especially Giacomo. He has two certifications, Italian Wine Professional, and Italian Wine Scholar. He knows his Italian vino, and his passion is old wines. Why not include them in our opportunity for dinner in a Tuscan vineyard, a night under the stars?

Tempranillo Festival 2021

San Miniato is about an hour's drive south of Lucca. After we discussed our itinerary for the festival, it was unanimous… we didn't want Giacomo to drive back after the event. The easy solution became clear. We would stay overnight and completely enjoy the festival and scout out the area around San Miniato too.

The drive through the Tuscan countryside to the vineyard turned into a spectacular event. The rolling, yellow grassy hills, dotted with olive groves and rows of vines were abundant in every direction you looked. Streets lined with those amazing Italian cypress trees painted a serene, peaceful setting. Arriving at the vineyard with the windows ajar, you could hear the peacefulness of the moment. The only sound… the tires traveling over the gravel as we entered the vineyards parking lot.

As we walked to the entrance, we noticed lights strung and glowing between the rows of vines. The venue was enchanting. I've noticed photos of rows of tables set in a vineyard before on social media and always wanted to take part in an event like this. It's a dream come true—one of those items I could now check off my long bucket list. The excitement began to build.

While checking in, we discovered Eva had comped the entrance fee for the four of us, likely because of my connection with Paul. How amazing and Italian is that? Wine glasses were distributed to each of us, and the evening began. A staff member guided us to our table in between the vines and we settled in for a sensational evening. We began tasting some of their amazing wine—each one tasting better than the last as the night continued. At this point we tried the VignaLeNicchie Tempranillo Toscana IGT. After clinking glasses in a toast, the expression on our faces said it all. Heaven. Our eyes rolled in delight with the bold, rich, taste dancing in our mouths. The deep red saturated color is apparent. Giacomo describes the Beconcini Tempranillo Toscana Prephilloxera Vigna Le Nicchie as:

> "A very unique wine in Italy from San Miniato in Tuscany. Tempranillo's a grape variety native to Spain that makes full-bodied red wines (e.g.,

> Rioja). The Tempranillo found in Tuscany, often erroneously called Malvasia Nera, has similar characteristics to the original Spanish grape but exhibits unique characteristics to the Italian cultivation. The color of the wine is a deep ruby red with aromas of dark chocolate, black fruit, spices, and a hint of coffee. The taste of the wine is medium to full body with fine tannins, creamy texture with a long, savory finish." *(Giacomo, August 2021)*

The Tuscan beef appetizer assortment, huge Fiorentina Steaks grilled on the enormous barbeque accompanied with savory, soft baked potatoes topped off the perfection of the evening. This truly was a night to remember—great wine, delicious food, live music, enjoyed with good friends against a spectacular backdrop... just beyond words. Even under pandemic restrictions, Eva and Leonardo, along with their family and crew, created an amazing festival we will never forget. Meeting and taking photos with Eva completed the unforgettable celebration of the 2021 grape harvest of Tempranillo di Toscana. We long to participate in this event year after year.

> "Custodian of a secret–ancient like our land"
> "...Long live the Tempranillo, the grape harvest"
> *(Eva and Leo Beconcini, pietrobeconcini.com)*

❧ *Autunno,* Fall ❧

(September 21 - December 20)

Pisa
Ilene

Our good friend, Victoria lives in Florence. She's a lovely ex-pat from California, a tour guide, blogger, and author. It's fun to meet occasionally, and of course, always stay connected by WhatsApp, the go-to way to text in Europe. We discovered during one visit that none of us had ever climbed the Leaning Tower in Pisa. Yes, we'd all visited several times, but none of us made it up to the top of the tower.

With a break in the weather, we traveled to Pisa on November 5. We coordinated train schedules as Victoria would take the train from Florence to Pisa and we'd meet her at the station. With the sun out, we appreciated the chance to get out of the house.

From the San Rossore train stop, it's an easy, short walk to the Field of Dreams. Still a bit chilly, a quick stop at the first *café* became high on our list. Cappuccinos all around plus a little dolce and we're ready to roll. A bathroom pit stop as well. When needing a restroom in Italy, stop for a *caffè* or water. Any small purchase grants you the use of their facilities.

It's not possible to simply "show up at the Leaning Tower" and expect to be admitted right away. Unless, of course, you are visiting during the off season. We recommend that you purchase tickets ahead of time, before the visit. Several time slots are available each day for the tower, and you book them accordingly. Each timeslot only allows a certain number of people to climb the tower. There are 251 steps to the top and the climb takes approximately thirty minutes. We've heard it's not difficult, but some people report feeling dizzy or experience vertigo from the tight, spiral staircase.

We weren't exactly sure what to expect but the climb turned out nothing as I imagined. Gary often grumbles every time I want to climb a tower. If he's done it once already, there's no chance I can convince him to scale the same tower a second time. Not even for an extraordinary view. We're both excited and willing to take the experience of the Leaning Tower of Pisa.

While waiting for our turn to ascend, Gary noticed something right away. We're having trouble standing at the base of the tower—just standing in one place. We're already feeling a bit off kilter and losing our balance—and we haven't even begun the climb. When it became our turn, we took our time. When a group behind us caught up to us, we took a break and let them pass. We certainly didn't want to hold up anyone from their experience.

The old marble steps were visibly worn and creviced in the center from hundreds of years of use. Some parts of the climb became more difficult, and I couldn't quite figure out why. Subsequently, Gary hit the nail on the head. You can easily figure out the side of the tower you are currently on. The stairs are influenced by the lean of the tower. When we ascended on the "top side," the climb became more difficult than when on the side of the tower closest to the ground. It's difficult to explain but most definitely a weird experience.

Arriving at the first level, it's a bit daunting when you see there's only a slight guardrail to keep you from falling off the edge. Despite that, the views of the city of Pisa and surrounding Tuscany are breathtaking. The perspective of the Field of Miracles with the Cathedral and Baptistery below are photo-worthy. Yes, I took quite a few photos. Taking our time, we walked around the platform. I slid my hand along the cold stone of the tower, using it as a guide when walking up the steep side.

"You can feel the slant of the tower," I called out to Victoria and Gary as they are now behind me.

Gliding my fingertips along the bumpy, stone, white structure I call to mind the history of this iconic monument. The painstaking work it took to erect, the controversy right from the start with all the problems and issues. The men who persevered years and years later to carry out and complete it. The engineers who continually put forth the effort to counterbalance it, so it truly won't lean much more. I'm touching on history. I take a moment to take in all the emotions I'm feeling.

We climbed to yet another floor from this platform for even better views. I'm happy a cage type fencing encompassed this level.

With the day clear, we could see for miles. The seven large brass bells at this level correspond to each note of the musical scale. Today, they just function as decoration, but I imagine at one time they were used in both warnings and celebrations for the city of Pisa.

Standing this close, I'm quite happy I wasn't in danger of them going off.

We leisurely walked back to the train station, chatting about the experience. It's unanimous, we're all happy we finally made the climb and thoroughly enjoyed the adventure. Parting ways at the station, Victoria headed back to Florence while we waited for our train to Lucca.

৯ Sesto Fiorentino ৶

Every few months, we visit our friends in Sesto Fiorentino, a town just outside of Florence. This couple owned the hotel we would always stay at when in Florence. This family came to our rescue when we left Bari after twenty-four hours in February 2017. It's a long story but we made the best of it by changing our plans and headed to Florence. Enter Angelina and Giuseppe.

They took us in and sheltered us. A bit too dramatic? We booked a room in their hotel while trying to find our apartment. They also became our good friends. Just before the pandemic hit, due to health conditions and perhaps their age too, they sold the hotel and moved closer to their son in Sesto Fiorentino.

ଓ

Arranging a day with Fernando, their son, Gary checked the train schedule, deciding which train we would take in the morning. While watching a little television the night before, we saw warnings when checking our phones about a transportation strike on social media. The ex-pats in Lucca play host to several Facebook groups and this kind of information is shared all the time. Grateful for the heads up, we texted Fernando that we'll check the train app in the morning and give him our update.

Turning off the alarm on his phone, Gary checked his app the very first thing.

"Doesn't show any issues, let's attempt the trip."

The train station is a brief twenty-minute walk from our apartment, and we arrived in plenty of time for Gary to use the machine and buy our tickets. Not sure what time we'd return to Lucca, we decided to buy one-way tickets. The train arrived, the trip uneventful, and we walked to their apartment upon arrival at the Sesto Fiorentino station.

Greeting us with big smiles, we know they are happy to see us again. Long ago, they owned a hotel and lived in London for several years, so they speak English quite well. Thank goodness as Gary and I are still not at the level of a full conversation in Italian. The coffee and sweets appeared on the table before I'd even set down my pocketbook.

After about two hours, I asked Gary to check his train app to see what times we need to consider for our return to Lucca. Gary pulled out his phone and after a flick of his finger opening his screen, he threw me a concerning look.

I paused my conversation with Angelina, "What's wrong?"

Gary turned his phone so I could see his screen. Without my glasses, all I could decipher is a sea of red across the screen in several places.

"Oh no, it's happening," I said out loud.

We know there's a bus we could take to Lucca, but we don't know anything about where to find it or even where to buy tickets in this town. The *tabaccheria* usually only sells local bus tickets.

We scrambled to help clean up while hastily gathering our things. We expressed our regrets for running out but there's a possibility there was one train left before the strike went into effect. It's a fair bet we wouldn't make it, but we should try. Air kisses thrown, we began sprinting toward the train station. Arriving, we try and catch our breaths. Gary purchased two tickets, but we are unsure by the display board if the train will actually stop at our station. His app was confusing and difficult to read with all the red notifications. A bit bewildered, we just stood there… not sure what we could or should do next.

We called Fernando to ask about the bus, but we reached his voicemail. Looking inside the station and prepared to use our best Italian, we couldn't find anyone. We decided to just wait for the train. Sitting on the bench, my right foots tapping… wondering. A few people gather and glance at their watches. *Ahh, they must be wondering if the train is coming too.* A reflection of light far down on the track caught my attention. I squinted to see what might be causing the glare. I smiled when I made out the front of a train headed our way.

Stopping at the station, we boarded and noticed there are no seats available, so we elected to stand by the doors. *There are more people than usual on this train, I think to myself.* We overheard a few young girls discussing the *treno*, train and ask if they thought this train would stop at Santa Maria Novella. In unison shoulders raised. Either they didn't understand English, or they just didn't know the answer. Our destination was Santa Maria Novella, the main station in Florence, allowing us to transfer to another traveling to Lucca.

When the train stopped at the next station, we popped our heads outside and saw a female Trenitalia employee dressed in blue with red trim. When we asked, she informs us this train won't take us to Santa Maria Novella, but we could exit at the next station and take the tram. We are familiar with the tram in Florence and enjoyed using it to pick up Ally and Brett when they came to visit us when we stayed there. The tram's a great new addition to transportation in Florence. Especially using it to go to the airport.

People were bombarding the female employee with questions and another employee joined her on the platform. The man spoke loudly, and they began bantering back and forth. I think this strike was affecting their day—and not in a good way. The train is running late because travelers stepped off, gathering on the platform next to the train, holding the doors open. Travelers are talking over one another blasting questions about how to arrive at their destinations. The train car was filled with loud, shrilling Italian and my head was spinning from all the noise. It became chaotic, to say the least. I scanned the train and instantly felt for a woman who had, I assume, her elderly father with her. He didn't appear to be able to walk well and seemed a bit unstable. She, too, wanted to reach Santa Maria Novella.

At the next stop, a crowd of us exited the train and headed down the steps. I offered to carry the woman's packages so she could attend to her father. Down at street level, we all walked over to the tram station and waited. Just a few moments later, the tram appeared and at least twenty of us boarded the tram.

I found a seat, but when seeing the woman and her father, I offered my seat to him, and he accepted it with a smile and whispered, *"Grazie."* He looked tired, and so was I.

In an instant it dawned on me that we'd boarded the tram without a ticket. It arrived so quickly after walking to the station, I had completely forgotten to buy one. With only a few stops to the main station where everyone must exit, we should have purchased one and we were incorrect for traveling this way. My only consolation—the other twenty or so people didn't buy one either. However, it didn't make our actions correct. Perhaps they had a pass or already bought their tickets ahead of time.

Arriving at the last stop in Centro in this direction, we all disembarked and made our way to the train station. It was the local line on strike and by the time we arrived at Santa Maria Novella, we secured a train to Lucca. It was a short day but we are tired. Arriving back at the apartment, we both plopped on the couch in exhaustion.

As we always say, things can change at a moment's notice, and you must remain flexible. When we left in the morning, we knew there was the possibility of a strike, but sometimes it doesn't materialize. We adapted and overcame. It's life in Italy, and not always so easy.

Daily Life

Sometime in September, a lovely woman from Florida contacted us on the blog letting us know she's moving to Italy. More importantly—she's moving to Lucca. After corresponding back and forth through email, we finally met. Full of energy, Joanne is a complete delight. We made plans to do events together as Joanne's quite the outdoors person. I'm amazed at her energy level to go on hiking trips each week. She's quite the adventurous one and this has the earmarks of a fun friendship.

After months of searching, Joanne decided on the apartment just down the street from us. Her apartment's beautiful but also a fifty-nine-step climb to the front door—no elevator in her building. It's brutal to visit her but she also has an unusual find in Lucca—a terrace. Her terrace faces the beautiful San Francisco church and a lovely piazza with the same name. It's funny because so many Americans live on our street, they've nicknamed Via del Fosso as "ex-pat ally." In total, I think there are about six or seven of us living along this beautiful street in Centro Storico.

ℭℜ

Through friends at English Monday, we heard about adult education classes that are provided by the City of Lucca. CPIA stands for *Centro Provinciale per I'istruzione Adult* conducts various classes at different levels throughout the week. I convince Gary we need to attend. Are you wondering how I convinced Gary? I apprised him of the cost.

"This year-long class will not hinder your wine budget, Gary. It won't even put a dent in it."

At EUR 20,00 per person for the school year, it's a screaming deal. It doesn't have the charm of taking lessons in a villa but it will tackle our language learning endeavor in a more pocket-friendly way.

We began CPIA in the middle of October and, immediately, fell in love with our teacher, Sara. We believe Sara's the head of the Italian learning courses, but don't quote me on it. She has a great personality, and you can tell she loves what she does. Our class began with about twenty-five people in it, including Gary and me. There were adults from Morocco, Mali, Sri Lanka, Albania, Iran, and just us two *Americani.* Yes, Gary and I were the only two Americans in this Pre-A1 level class. Sara's going to need a great deal of patience. How does one even begin to teach a language to a group of adults who don't know what she's saying? Well, when she slows down her conversation to a snail's pace, I could kind of understand the gist, most of the time, of what she's saying. Some of the students spoke some Italian already as they've lived in Italy for a while. When I'm confused, I give Gary a little poke in his back as he sits in front of me.

"She said it's important, do you understand what she's saying?" I whispered to Gary on more than one occasion.

Sara speaks *un po,* a little, English. It's funny because when involved in teaching something, and not sure we were all understanding the meaning, she tried to explain further using the little English she knew. *Professoressa* Sara would look at either Gary or me to confirm the English words she said. I would say ninety percent of the time she had the word correct.

One of the funniest things happened often to only me in class. Masks those days were mandatory and with them on, it became difficult to hear, understand, and comprehend Sara teaching. As I've mentioned before, masks hinder my ability to learn. My assigned seat was behind Gary in the second seat of a row, close to the front of the class. I was always listening intensely. Perhaps too keenly.

I guess the frown on my face from listening so zealously, along with my mask covering, inevitably lead *Professoressa* Sara to say, *"E-lain-a, capisco?"*

Most of the time I replied, *"Si, si, si,"* or occasionally I had to admit and say, *"No, non capisco."*

Gary and I chuckled at each instance because we knew it had to do with my frowning or expressions and she would associate it with me not understanding. I'd since tried to relax monitoring so hard as I certainly don't want the wrinkles on my forehead to become permanent.

We enjoyed our twice-a-week classes, two hours each day, and riding our bicycles. The school is located outside the wall, but not distant. It only gave the feeling of being far when it rained. Gary and I hadn't mastered the Italian way of riding a bicycle. These Italians are masters. They can ride a bicycle while holding an umbrella, smoking a cigarette, and most of the time, talking on their cellphone. Such coordination.

☙

A most pleasant surprise came when contacted by Suzanne and Marcus from Long Beach, New York. They just finished our book and commented on one of our recent blog posts. Before we even met them, Gary, and I both knew we liked them. Isn't it funny how that can happen? This young couple is moving to an area just outside Lucca, building their own home, and bringing their three large dogs and a parrot.

After informing them about English Monday, we decided when they arrived and settled in a bit, they would come to meet this group of people—including us. After corresponding with them for a while, finally meeting them became a moment I'll always treasure. Almost like a first kiss… They are both amazing and we've enjoyed the opportunity to know them better. It's always fun to do excursions together, enjoy dinner at one of our homes, or run into them in the streets when they venture into Lucca Centro.

☙

If you recall, we were supposed to return to Arizona at the end of October. We booked our first apartment rental when arriving on April 1 until October 29 with the beginning of Lucca's Comic and Games. Our apartment owner, Ricardo already rented the apartment to a family coming for the event. People come to this event every year like clockwork and quite a few Airbnb rentals in Lucca Centro rent to the same people each year.

However, when I made the declaration in the middle of May, that Lucca became my "perfect Italian town," we needed to break the bad news to Ricardo that we wouldn't stay until October. We needed to find a long-term rental. I don't like conflict and try to avoid it at all costs. Choosing my words carefully, we told him we needed to find a long-term apartment as we've decided to remain permanently in Lucca. He expressed his disappointment but understood. I'm sure most rentals lost a great deal of income when Italy shut down. Vacation rentals remained empty as no tourists were able to enter the country.

After securing a long-term rental in Centro, Gary and I both decided to postpone our scheduled October trip home until the beginning of December and return to family and friends for the holidays. After all, we just committed to living full-time in Italy. With changes made with the airlines, we planned to enjoy Thanksgiving, an American tradition, in Italy.

☙

Wanting to try shopping at a store outside the wall, I pulled out my phone and searched Google maps. Carrefour's a large store like a Walmart or Target. It carries a little bit of everything and is one of those one-stop shopping experiences. Gary and I've ridden our bicycles before, but I want to bring my "grandma" trolly grocery cart and pick up quite a few larger things. Items that can't be carried easily on a bicycle. Heavy, larger size laundry soap and a six-pack of toilet paper are on my list.

Several small autobuses travel through and outside the historic center of Lucca. Each enters and exits through a different *porta* or gate in Centro Storico. The Blu LAM autobus travels east and west while the Rosso LAM follows a more southwest to northeast route. The Verdi LAM travels north and south. It's easy and cheap to buy tickets at the tobacco shop. The cost of EUR 1,50 entitles you to ninety minutes of travel time, and if you can make it to your destination and back within the timeframe—bingo, that's all it will cost you. If I'm shopping, I normally need to buy two tickets, one for each way.

It's the Rosso LAM autobus I take from a bus stop close to our apartment out the northeastern porta close to Carrefour. The store's only a few miles from our apartment, but taking the little bus is fun and I enjoy the experience.

This store is unique on two floors. The first floor consists of groceries but also has a diversified kitchen department with items such as dishes, glasses, pots, and pans. A small garden department, clothing, shoes, patio furniture, and sporting goods complete the first-floor selection. I'm being a bit general, but you understand the idea. The escalator takes you up to the second floor where you'll find the hardware department, bedding and towels, books, and appliances—ranging from small to large items. The prices here are reasonable, and I like the one-stop shopping. If we owned a car, it would be easier. For now, we take several trips rather than the true one-stop scenario. It's all right, we've adapted well.

☙

In this same area, we recently bought my new MacAir from Media World. Shopping's a different experience in Italy than in the States. I'm not sure if it's an Italy or European thing, but you need confidence in the item you want to purchase. Return policies are peculiar. Contrary to what you are used to, it's rare you will receive a refund for items returned to a store in Italy. Within the time allowed, you can return the merchandise, but for a *buono*, store credit—not a credit on your credit card or cash returned.

I found this out as it never occurred to me when I bought my new computer, it would not bear a standard keyboard, but an Italian one. I panicked. I didn't want to open the box because I know from experience once you open a box, it's a different ballgame. I went on the Internet to do some research. Gary's confident Apple wouldn't make individual keyboards for different countries, as that would be counterproductive. *But what could be the difference, I wondered?* Recognize, I'm a die-hard Windows user trying to convert to Apple. This fact alone might send me over the edge. *Why do I do this to myself?*

After a few days, Gary and I concluded I need to just open the box and check it out. Nothing showed what the keyboard would look like online—and the search became futile. Excited but apprehensive, I broke the seal and opened the computer box. Other than the different control, option, and command keys, I observed only a few minor differences. The question mark and some other punctuation keys turned out in a different spot, but nothing major. What I noticed right off the bat? Separate keys for a euro and lira symbol, as well as "e" accent keys. Interesting. It wasn't quite as bad as I expected. Now I need to find the time to understand this computer and an entirely different system. *Fun, fun, fun... again why do I do this to myself?*

ଓ

Rainy days were quite frequent, and the temperatures dropped. All my pretty annual flowers on the terrace were starting to give up their color. They wouldn't last much longer. I'm surprised they've lasted this long but I attribute it to the *sole,* sun still covering most of our terrace in the afternoon.

ଓ

I've previously mentioned how time flies when you're older. I never understood it when my parents would talk about it. It didn't make sense to me, but it does now. A lot of things my parents said to me as a child are very clear—crystal clear now that I'm older. I wish I could tell them, "I get it now," but they're no longer with us. Sad but I think both would've appreciated hearing those words from me.

I feel, however, that days pass more rapidly in Italy than when we are in the States. Life is just different in Italy. It's not because there's nothing to do here as we are plenty busy. It's not the fact that I rise later, because I don't, usually hitting the ground about seven-thirty in the morning. Unless I'm a bit lazy and wait for the eight o'clock church bells to ring. It's a sound Gary and I love hearing throughout Italy. There's a sense of peace and calm when we hear them, I guess.

However, when I hear the noon bells each day, they remind me the day's half over, or at least a good chunk of time has already passed in the day. I usually let out a deep, loud sigh. Gary expects the audible sound from me each and every day. I've still so many things I want to accomplish. In the big scheme of things, it doesn't matter if I finish a project today or tomorrow, or even next week. Yet I try to keep to my schedule, and the church bells are just a lovely reminder I'm either succeeding or not on the particular day.

☙

I couldn't wait to tell Gary the new James Bond movie, *No Time to Die,* was playing at one of the local movie theaters inside the wall. Viewing in English with Italian subtitles would be fun, and I wanted to go. We especially wanted to see this movie. Although I'm not a huge Bond fan, some of it took place in Matera, a town we love and visited before. It's the twenty-fifth film in the James Bond series produced by Eon Productions.

Checking with our friend Joel, he wanted to attend too. None of us ever experienced a movie theater in Italy before. Curious, each of us truly didn't know what to expect. I bought the tickets online for EUR 8,50 each, and we met Joel just before showtime in front of the theater. On a rainy Monday night, we saw lots of our friends from English Monday. I guess it's a favorite indoor activity for many on such a nasty evening.

Entering the theater, we must show our "green pass." The next stop… the concession stand. *Oh yes*—they sell popcorn at the movies in Italy. I was a happy camper. Other snacks and drinks appeared to be available, but I did notice our grandchildren would be extremely disappointed… there were no American "ices" were for sale. Paying EUR 2,50 for a small popcorn, we found our seats.

Cinema Moderno opened in 1924 and is incredibly beautiful. In pristine condition, the red velvet wide comfortable chairs matched the long, gathered red velvet curtains on the stage. Gold cording adorned the curtains, and I was quite taken aback by the beauty of this theater. A painted or frescoed ceiling added to the ambiance and elegance of the vast room. Several small balconies like you would see in an opera house adorned the sides.

Two strange things happened while at the theater. The first one, the movie started on time—not "Italian time," but exactly at the advertised time, surprising all of us. The other occurred halfway through the movie. The large screen went completely black, and after a quick moment, the overhead lights were illuminated. Sitting in the middle between Gary and Joel, I switched my head back and forth looking at each of them, almost like watching a tennis tournament. My puzzled expression said it all without any words spoken. Both shrugged their shoulders—clearly neither of them had a clue what was going on. I thought there may be a power outage due to the *brutto tempo,* bad weather but unexpectedly a notification appeared on the screen. It turned out to be a five-minute intermission, and the countdown began. The movie was only about two and a half hours long, but I guess a break might be needed.

The movie didn't disappoint me, and the scenes filmed in Matera appeared at the beginning of the movie. I nudged Gary with my elbow when I spotted several places where they filmed in the city—we knew exactly where they were. The chase sequence with Bond driving an Aston Martin DB5 through the tiny streets of Matera was tremendous. I enjoyed reading the Italian subtitles and picking out several words I understood. I caught myself paying more attention to the subtitles and translating it in my head. Several times I needed to pull myself back to watching the movie itself. It was a great evening, and the popcorn wasn't half bad.

∽ Stop and Taste the Vino ∼

Gary

I'm admittedly an Italian wine snob. Growing up in New York I began drinking my grandfather's homemade Italian red vino at the age of twelve. Mind you, I wasn't drinking straight wine. At dinnertime, my grandfather would pour half a glass of coca cola and fill the rest with wine.

Unlike some homemade wines, my grandfather's wine tasted pretty darn good. I remember finding the key to his wine cellar at the age of fifteen. I would sneak downstairs, open the cellar, fill a little wine into an empty cola bottle and go out with my friends.

Visiting my grandparents one Sunday, my grandfather casually walked up to me, putting his arm around my shoulder, and took me aside. In a soft-spoken voice, he asked if I liked his wine.

Shrugging my shoulders with my head looking down at my feet, I meekly replied "Yes."

With a slight grin on his face, he told me to make sure to put the key back in its proper place and to also remember to rinse out the jug when I'm finished with it. I raised my head and I gazed up into his eyes. He hugged me and told me not to say anything to the others, it would be our secret.

Our secret stayed between us until his death. When Pop died so did his winemaking expertise. No one else in the family showed an interest in learning the craft of winemaking—including me. To this day, the fact I never learned from Pop how to make Italian wine gnaws at me. Looking back, I know this will remain one of the great disappointments of my life.

ᏡᏕ

When we lived in Phoenix, my favorite place to shop for wine was a store called Total Wine. They sold wines, liquors, and beer from all over the world. Their selection was second to none and the staff were very friendly and helpful. Needless to say, I became known throughout the store as the Italian wine guy. On a few occasions, while browsing the Italian wine section, a staff member would approach me and ask if I could help a customer find a particular Italian wine or, one I might recommend in its place. I guess when you spend as much time as I did in the Italian wine section you're noticed. Even the store manager knew me by name and would ask for my opinion from time to time. My favorite day… when the new Total Wine catalog came out.

Italian wines are broken down into four designations. They are DOCG, DOC, IGT, and VDT. Without boring you with what each designation means, I did an extensive post on the blog about this subject. Remember, it's all about taste, *your* taste not mine or the experts. Good wine comes in all designations.

The very first rule on selecting wine I will impart to you—there are no set-in-stone rules. If you taste a wine you like, no matter what wine designation it's given—enjoy it. The second rule, all good wines are expensive—that's hogwash. I've tasted wines costing upwards of EUR 200,00 per bottle and enjoyed them less than wines costing under EUR 10,00 per bottle. The third rule—the wines age. Here again, not all older wines are to my liking. My taste tends to gravitate to mid-aged wines.

I must admit, before moving to Italy most of my wine selections were based on price especially if I liked the flavor of a specific bottle. I would buy the same three or four bottles every week never veering to something different. Everything changed the day we became friends with Gianna and Giacomo. Giacomo's a certified Italian wine expert, one step removed from a sommelier, and Gianna, while not certified, is very knowledgeable as well. For some reason, Giacomo decided to take me under his wing and broaden my wine horizons. He's introduced me to old wines that in the past I shied away from. On the other hand, I introduced him to the pleasures of younger wines and where they fit into the enjoyment of wine. Today, when we all go out together, Giacomo will look at the wine list first, and next ask me for my recommendation. We normally come to a compromise and order a wine we all could enjoy.

At this point, I want to introduce a different category of wine. It's called *sfuso*. What's *sfuso* you ask? It's the name for bulk wine, you know, wine sold in five-liter boxes or bottles. Before COVID hit you were able to take your bottles to where they sold *sfuso* and fill the bottles up yourself. Today *sfuso* is either prepackaged in five-liter boxes or they pour it fresh for you in a bottle they must supply.

Most stores selling *sfuso* offer five or more types of wine. They offer sparkling, white, or red wines. These wines are not home brews but come from some of the best vineyards in Italy. We've enjoyed reds such as Montalcino Rosso, Chianti, Bulgari, and Sangiovese, and whites like Chardonnay and Vermentino which are all very good. The best part of buying *sfuso's* the price. We buy a Montecarlo Rosso from one of our favorite restaurants, Cicci's, at EUR 25,00 for a five-liter box… breaking down to EUR 3,85 for a 750 ml bottle. We've even found a place outside of Lucca with a delicious *sfuso* for EUR 10,00 for a five-liter box. Occasionally, this has become our everyday wine. We cook with it, and we will sit on our terrazzo enjoying a glass while watching the sunset. As I mentioned earlier, the cost and designation of wine doesn't matter. *What matters?* Your taste and what you like. As the saying goes; you can lead a horse to water, but you can't make him drink it. I hope I pointed you in the right direction, the rest's up to you. As we say in Italy, *cin cin,* pronunciation [chin-chin]. This is the Italian word for "cheers." Italians either use the word *"salute"* or *"cin cin"* and usually followed by *"alla nostra salute,"* which means "to your health."

Lucca Comic and Games

Lucca, the home of the Anfiteatro, *le mura,* Puccini, one hundred churches, gorgeous palazzos, and home to an epicenter of Lucca Comic and Games. Since 1996, on the last weekend in October for a four-day duration, this otherwise quiet town hosts the world's third largest convention of this kind. Tokyo, Japan, and San Diego, California rank numbers one and two. The Tokyo event is called "Comiket" while in San Diego, it's known as "Comic-Con."

Normally this show attracts over 400,000 attendees, but because of COVID restrictions, Lucca allowed only one-quarter of the normal numbers. I understand the fact that it's good for businesses and tax revenues but 100,000 people—let alone the 400,000 normally, make Lucca very crowded. The streets are packed, and it's almost impossible to get into most restaurants. Walking the streets also becomes nearly impossible. A mere fifteen-to-twenty-minute walk from one side of town to the other can take as much as forty-five minutes. Trains arriving in Lucca are crammed with those taking part in the event but enough of my whining because it's a sight to behold for everyone. In retrospect, it's great for Lucca.

The convention is divided into Lucca Comics and Lucca Games. The comic segment of this event is dedicated to comics and animations. Meanwhile, the games division is more about role-playing or performance art to board games, from medieval games represented in this type of historical setting, etc.

It all begins about three weeks before the convention starts. Huge tents are erected for the exhibits in most piazzas and open spaces. Some of these tents are big enough to fit a football field inside of them and include a heating system and electric hookups. These reserved areas host games, exhibitions, and competitions.

This year, 2021, the event opened on October 29 to a limited number of visitors each day, again because of COVID restrictions. Those of us staying in town, are stocked up on groceries and hunkered down for the duration. We ventured outside during Comic and Games briefly—just to glimpse at the elaborate costumes. If you've never experienced one of these events, I'll try my best to describe it for you. Picture, if you will, thousands of people dressed up as their favorite comic, game, or movie characters strolling through the historic streets of Lucca. Some costumes are more elaborate than others, but all are creative and amazing. Not only are they dressed like their favorite characters, but most will pose and act for tourists to take photos.

Lucca comes alive when the Comic and Games event is in town. Simply walking the wall, you'll see hundreds of characters dressed in full regalia putting on a show for all to see. This year we watched Darth Vader equipped with a light saber walking with legendary Jedi Master, Obi-Wan Kenobi, and a young Anakin Skywalker. Represented also… Mario Brothers, Belle and the Beast, Cruella de Vil, Squid game guards, and Money Heist robbers. We recognized some costumes but just couldn't pinpoint them by name. Some are incredibly elaborate and elegant. Two stunning women appeared coordinated in matching tight silk, colorful costumes adorned with amazing headdresses. One of the women dressed in orange with purple flower accents and the other in yellow and white. When Ilene took their photo, they stopped and posed. Later, on social media, she showed me the same two ladies with wings spread out like butterflies. The attention to detail is remarkable. Some accessories strike us as impressive as the costumes themselves. Families even dressed together in coordinating outfits, including some pooches.

Our first-time visiting Lucca during Comic and Games had been in 2019 when we caught the last two days of this extravaganza. I remember telling Ilene that I would want to vacate Lucca during this event because of the crowds and confusion. For the most part, many of the ex-pats I spoke with who live here said they leave town because it's a zoo. Now mind you when COVID's no longer a factor and the number of visitors get back to normal, I might sing a different tune. One hundred thousand attendees weren't a problem, but four hundred thousand people might be a different story. Maybe Ilene and I will just take a week away from Lucca and avoid the throngs of visitors like others do or maybe we'll dress up as our favorite characters and join in the festivities. Then again, I don't think so, but you never know with us.

❧ An Anniversary of a Different Kind ☙
Ilene

I became extremely busy at the beginning of November preparing to celebrate our anniversary. Not our wedding anniversary, but the publication of our first book, *Our Italian Journey* would turn one year old on November 19. Once again, time has flown by in the blink of an eye. Gary and I talked about how we would celebrate this momentous occasion and decided on some fun with a contest with gift cards for winners.

A few correct answers fetched from the book would be a fun challenge. Some comments on social media also agreed the book couldn't possibly be in existence and published a year ago—wasn't it perhaps just six months ago? Some unexpected comments brought me to tears with kind words about how our adventure has led them to grasp life and create their own journey. Not as drastic as selling it all and moving to another country but following a dream. Listening to their heart instead of their head and doing something they were always reluctant or scared to do. To think we influenced a few souls deeply moved me. The thought brought a few tears to the corner of my eye, but it also brought a smile to my face.

The giveaway was fun and successful. Gary and I opened a bottle of Prosecco and celebrated. We never, e-v-e-r considered writing a book, and yet a year later people were requesting to meet us—just to chat and share their stories with us. We've won a few awards and have been interviewed several times, and close friends have encouraged us to go through this process again to complete our story with this book. Life takes you down the most unexpected paths. If you're still mulling a dream of yours, but haven't yet acted on it, embrace it the next chance you get. Opportunity comes knocking once, maybe twice… don't waste the next chance. You deserve to live your best life.

~ Thanksgiving Italian Style ~

With our kitchen being small, we asked only Joel, Gianna, and Giacomo to join us for the festivities. Gary and I took charge of the turkey, stuffing, and my famous cheesecake. In case the cheesecake failed, Joel was given the task of bringing a backup dessert. Gianna and Giacomo would complete the feast with side dishes and wine. Menu set, we're almost ready to roll.

A trip to Tuccori Mariano, our favorite *macelleria,* butcher shop became top on the list. After all, what's Thanksgiving without a turkey? This family-owned establishment is our favorite place to buy meats, cheeses, and prepared dishes. Located on Via Santa Croce, their lasagna and eggplant parmesan are so good, that we prefer to buy it from them rather than make it ourselves. One of their *formaggio,* Pecorino Romano cheeses covered in hay is simply scrumptious and a favorite of ours.

One of the best things about this store—the husband-and-wife team of Graziana and Mariano. Graziana is originally from Canada and speaks English. Her husband, Mariano does not. He mainly takes care of the meat area, and I love watching and listening to Gary and Mariano chat over the counter about meat.

During one of our first visits, we revealed to Graziana, that Gary's first job as a young man was in a butcher shop. When she conveyed this to her husband, his eyes lit up in delight. Normally when we go in the store for something for the BBQ grill, Gary will point to a nice piece of meat in the case. Occasionally, Mariano will look at Gary with a slight tilt of his head. In Italian, he'll ask Graziana to find out what we are planning to use the cut of meat for—how is Gary planning to cook it? Gary will tell Graziana who conveys Gary's thoughts to her husband. Sometimes it's quite hilarious when Mariano shakes his head, side to side… "No" to Gary after his wife repeats Gary's reply to him in Italian. Inevitably, he will point to another cut of meat, and Gary will always defer to his judgment and agree. Gary hasn't quite figured out all the various cuts available in Lucca as they are very different from those offered in the States.

☙

Back to Thanksgiving. For this occasion, we stopped at Tuccori to order a turkey—a whole turkey. Graziana advised we should obtain a ten to twelve-pound bird for the number of people we've invited and can pick it up two days before.

The meal planning came together, except something is missing per Gary. He insisted he wanted jellied cranberry sauce. Several trips to different markets did not provide us with any jellied sauce. We found others available, but not quite what Gary wanted for his American Thanksgiving dinner. Being a good wife, I searched the Internet as a last resort. Time was running out and I wanted to satisfy Gary's main request. I found online Gary's favorite brand, Ocean Spray, jellied. At EUR 9,00 a can with a minimum purchase of four required, Gary would enjoy his staple for dinner. Of course, I grumbled the entire time paying such an extraordinary amount for a side dish usually costing less than fifty cents a can in the States during the holiday. We did, however, sell one can to a fellow ex-pat to recuperate some expenses. This is what we do in Lucca, we help each other out with our unique needs. Regardless, it's the little things that make all the difference in the world.

☙

Gary always reminds me of the Thanksgiving we celebrated when we still owned our home in Phoenix, Arizona. Cooper, one of our grandsons, loves jellied cranberry sauce… just like Gary. Flashback to this Thanksgiving, I was determined to step it up a notch and made Martha Stewarts' fresh cranberry salsa. Cranberries, tiny orange pieces, and spices created a holiday aroma throughout the house. When it came time to sit down to eat, Cooper glared over at Gary with his eyes wide open along with a puzzled, and frightened look. I recollect Cooper being about five years old at the time and his expression of fear and bewilderment. As plates were passed and filled, Gary opened the pantry door and brought out a can of Ocean Spray jellied cranberry sauce. Cooper watched Gary's every move and beamed with delight when he saw the familiar white can. Thanksgiving had been saved for Gary and Cooper.

ଓ

When we arrived to claim our turkey, Graziana informs Gary, that Mariano has a special one picked out just for him. It's a thirteen-pound beauty and hand selected just for us. There's something extraordinary about shopping in a store like this. Yes, it's so nice being greeted personally when you first walk into the store, and yes, it's so nice to experience the extra special feeling that these wonderful people appreciate your shopping with them. Choosing them over someone else or a major grocery store. We knew this family was special—right from the first time we entered their shop.

Thanksgiving arrived and Gary's in charge in the *cucina,* kitchen. Gary and his mom, Elaine, always prepared and cooked the turkey at our house. As we gaze at the bird all cleaned up and stuffed, Gary and I give each other a puzzled look. The lightbulb goes on. Will the turkey even fit in our little oven? We both crossed our fingers as Gary slid the heavy pan with our dinner into the *forno*, oven. It fit but we notice the metal oven rack began bowing a bit in the center from the weight. Ovens in Italy contain the flimsiest oven racks. Even my Le Creuset Dutch oven pot causes the rack to give more than I would prefer. After a few bastings, we decided to move the rack to the lowest position so as not to lose the bird to an unfortunate flight.

When all was said and done, the holiday turned out so nice. We enjoyed our friends, some very good food and wine, and considered ourselves very blessed. The turkey was moist and delicious and perhaps one of the best I've ever enjoyed. The entire holiday was successful, even my cheesecake.

Ilene's New York Cheesecake

Tools needed:
9-inch spring form pan
Flat lasagna-type dish
NOTE: ** Bake one day ahead **

Ingredients:
4 – 8-ounce packages of cream cheese, softened
1 – 16-ounce container of sour cream
1 – teaspoon good vanilla extract
5 – large eggs
2 – tablespoons corn starch
1½ cups sugar
1 – teaspoon fresh lemon juice
½ cup butter, room temperature (almost liquid state)
1 – can Comstock cherries in juice (optional)

Directions:

1. Preheat oven to 375°
2. Combine everything except eggs in a standing mixer. You can make this without the mixer, it just takes more time.
3. When all is combined, add eggs one at a time, slowly until each egg is incorporated.
4. Place your empty spring pan into the empty large lasagna pan. This will be your water bath to properly cook the cheesecake. Make sure your spring pan is properly locked with the bottom fitting snugly.
5. Pour the cheese mixture into the spring pan.
6. Add enough tap water to just the lasagna pan to come halfway up the side of the spring pan. This is called a water bath. The water will keep the cheesecake moist while baking.
7. Cook for about one hour. Keep checking to make sure the top doesn't get too brown. If it starts to get dark, lay a piece of aluminum foil loosely on the top

of the spring pan. It is common for the cheesecake to crack a bit on the top, this is normal. Insert a toothpick in the center to check if done. It should come out clean. Depending on where you live and your elevation, it sometimes can take another fifteen to thirty minutes to achieve a clean toothpick test. Do not overcook! A little moisture on the toothpick is all right.

8. Carefully remove the spring pan from the water bath and cool it on a rack on the counter. Do not open the spring pan. When completely cool, cover with plastic wrap and keep in the refrigerator overnight.
9. Remove the spring pan when ready to serve. Can serve plain or with a can of Comstock cherries on top. Perhaps a little sprinkle of powdered sugar on the cherries too.

Inverno, Winter

(December 21 - March 20)

Arezzo
Ilene

One of our favorite towns in Tuscany, and at one time a top contender for our "perfect town"—the medieval town of Arezzo. We thoroughly enjoyed staying thirty days in this town. It's one of our most enjoyable memories as we attended the medieval event, the Giostra del Saracino. The Giostra is a medieval revelry, filled with costumed ceremonies affiliated with the historic competition. It wasn't just attending the one event, we became part of the neighborhood, as our rental apartment existed in the Porta Crucifera district. This event takes place twice a year. The third Saturday in June and the first Sunday in September. We both enjoyed and treasure the fond memories of this month and the people we met in Arezzo.

It turns out Arezzo's also known for its Christmas market located in Piazza Grande. Several from our English Monday group wanted to take a day trip to enjoy this special event during this time of year. Gary and I expressed our excitement and agreed to join them. Returning to Arezzo, even just to visit for the day, would be wonderful. Ready with our hats and gloves, we were prepared for the chilly evening. The market comes alive especially in the evening with the display of digital lighting cast upon the medieval homes found around the piazza. The trip included a walking tour of Arezzo and even though Gary and I lived there for thirty days, a decent amount of time, we wanted to learn more about the city. Re-experiencing several special places, especially the *duomo* became a treat.

After the tour, we broke into smaller groups while Gary and I wanted to quickly say hello to our favorite couple, Luciana and Valerio who own the *il fruttivendolo,* a fruit and vegetable store around the corner from Piazza Grande. A few of our friends joined us and as we approached the store, Valerio recognized us right away. Unfortunately, Luciana wasn't there, and we told him to wish her well for us. We often think of this kind, wonderful couple as they treated us like family with a few Italian lessons thrown in.

Off to visit the market and find something to eat, we all decided to stay in the piazza, so Gary and I recommended one of our favorite restaurants, Ristorante La Lancia D'Oro. When we arrived and were seated, I asked if their daughter, Martina was working. When advised "No," I didn't give it another thought. We visited this restaurant often when staying in Arezzo and developed a friendship with the family. Maurizio, the father, won the Giostra many years ago and enjoyed showing us his photos, winning target, and actual lance.

As we enjoyed our *aperitivo*, the waiter came over, leaning slightly toward me, and whispered to me that Martina was on her way to see us. *"What?"* I couldn't believe it. I had goosebumps on my arms. What I also couldn't believe… Martina and her boyfriend, Nicolo, married and welcomed a little boy who stayed home with a sitter. A memorable photo taken of all of us, including Maurizio, Martina's father, completed the evening. Two years elapsed since we stayed in Arezzo, yet they remembered us.

As the sun set, darkness filled the piazza. The piazza turned into a magical display of color and light. Patterns of stars, snowflakes, and fleur-de-lis projected onto the buildings came alive with movement. The bright golds, royal purples, various blues, and rich red colors along with different patterns on each building brought the piazza to life.

With holiday music playing, the tone became set for an evening of festivities. Gary and I bought a cup of hot chocolate spiked with rum. We thought a little warmth might go a long way. When I spotted these huge Bavarian pretzels, I bought three for our little group to share. We all nibbled while investigating all the treasures for sale at each open cabin.

There wasn't a shortage of Christmas ornaments made in various materials and sizes. Handmade sweaters, gloves, and scarves appeared in every weight, pattern, and color. Cute stuffed animals, especially sheep and bears were in abundance with the sweetest embroidered faces. I thought of each young grandchild who would've liked to snuggle in bed for the night with one of them. Among other items offered for sale were blankets, mugs, and handmade jewelry. If you wanted a gift, you could've certainly found one there.

With departure time near, we returned to meet back at the bus. A few friends strutted new hats they bought, and everyone began sharing their new bargains with the group. We enjoyed being back in this town, and although it has a piece of my heart, it's not home.

Florence

Gary and I both reckoned it was about time to return to Florence. During earlier visits at this time of year, we enjoyed discovering all the Christmas decorations. Certainly, our favorite city would present itself with twinkling white lights strung from side to side on almost every street. Making a reservation for an overnight visit, we could enjoy the city and take in all the Christmas lights. The day turned into a little shopping spree, patronizing our favorite stores, and briefly reconnecting with friends.

As night fell, we bundled up for warmth and strolled the streets.

I quickly asked Gary, "How about a visit to La Rinascente Department Store and something to warm us while visiting their special rooftop restaurant?"

This store is a bit on the high-end side but the terrace on the roof offers a beautiful view of Florence. The prices are very reasonable, and the view can't be beaten. Unless you climb Brunelleschi's dome at the Santa Maria del Fiore Cathedral, but it takes a great deal of effort. Been there done that. Rinascente has an elevator and Gary thought it was a great idea.

Taking the escalator instead, we stopped at a few floors to check out some pretty clothes I spotted along the way. Peeking at the price tags, I sighed and determined they weren't in our budget. "*Andiamo,* Gary" and back on the escalator to the top we went. Arriving at the terrace, we found a table along the perimeter with great views of Piazza della Repubblica below, the large piazza with the carousel not far from the *duomo.* After looking over the menu, we each decided to order a glass of vino, and some warm *zuppa*, soup. It sounded like the perfect item to order, something to warm our old bones.

As we clinked glasses, I reached across the table and took Gary's hand in mine. With my grin and squeeze of his hand, I let Gary know my gratitude. We observed several other tables enjoyed by couples and families, there to enjoy the festive lights from this perspective too. We could see high up on the hills of Florence and the decorations down several streets. Photos were taken without question. Feeling content, we descended to the streets for more exploration.

The Arno River and Ponte Vecchio Bridge were our first stops. We stood and watched a video mapping movie displayed on the bridge, but different from the amazing Leonardo Da Vinci show we saw two years previously. If I recall, they did a Da Vinci tribute to honor the genius, 500 years after his death. We walked to the Ponte Vecchio and stopped. Without tourists, the bridge, practically empty, became a sight to behold. These areas are usually packed with people and difficult to maneuver. Not tonight. Not this year. Travel restrictions in Italia were still evident with the absence of tourists.

Passing the *duomo*, we headed for the other side of town back to the train station. We wanted to see the tree in Piazza Santa Maria Novella. In 2019, the tree stood unique, constructed of metal circles, intertwining in multiple colors with larger diameters at the base and smaller at the top. The various shades of blues and purples created a quilt-type look, very artsy and creative. As we arrived at the piazza, we paused, almost at the same time, and gave each other a glance. *What happened?* We both thought. The piazza was empty... vacant of all decorations—not even one. Stunned, the extra effort to walk to this area disappointed us. We both muttered, expressing our letdowns and emotions. Silently we walked back to the hotel for the night—an anticlimactic ending to our holiday spirit.

ଓ

With a late rise, Gary checked the train schedule for our return home. Home—this word, this feeling which keeps bringing a smile to my face. It's said a home is a feeling, not a place. It's a meaningful place inducing a sense of calmness and belonging. A home need not be static. It might lie where we grew up as children, but it can just as easily exist where we feel settled and begin a new life, full of possibilities. I know my heart has found its home when I think of Lucca.

ೋ Return to the States ೋ

You might be wondering why we haven't mentioned our trip back to the States—the one that should've taken place at the beginning of December. The nightmares we'd heard people experiencing with their travel plans hit us too. Emails from British Airways told us they canceled all their flights in and out of Pisa. We could change our itinerary and fly out of Rome to Heathrow but flying out of Pisa, our now preferred airport, wasn't possible. Perhaps I could have wrapped my head around this change if they would've just informed us of the reason—but none offered. A flight out of Rome would have meant added costs. Just flying to Heathrow would now entail two train tickets from Lucca to Florence, afterward Rome. We'd need to stay at the Hilton in Rome's airport because the flight was changed and scheduled for the wee hours of the morning. As you well know, this change would require us rising at the crack of dawn and reaching the terminal at three o'clock. Could we do it? Yes. Did we want to do it? No.

On the other hand, the icing on the cake? British Airways charged us added taxes. Because we used our points to fly on American, the taxes involved were reasonable. British Air, on the other hand, tripled those taxes to fly into Heathrow. How is this possible with tickets already bought? All the new changes would cost over USD 1,000.00 and we were annoyed. This, and the fact that we're enrolled and attending school at CPIA weekly, required us to stop and reevaluate the situation. Was there any easy answer? It turned out disappointing for us, family, and friends. We would wait and return next year. Travel restrictions might be less of a headache, we assume, and might just become easier. Decisions were made and disappointment set in.

An Italian Invitation

We received a text from our landlord Maurizio, he and his wife would like to invite us for a few hours to their home just outside of Lucca for *caffè.* With our acceptance of the invitation, he would come to pick us up in his car and we scheduled to meet him at our *porta,* San Jacopo. It's always nice to see him again as he's such a gentle, soft-spoken man. Struggling, I began to speak to him in Italian from my location in the back seat, remembering he told me back in the summer that… "Come January, we will speak only Italian." He chuckled and told me it was too difficult to try and understand me, let's speak English. I guess I haven't improved as much as I'd hoped. After a few twists and turns through the outer streets of Centro Lucca and over the Serchio River, we arrived ten minutes later at their home in the countryside. It sits up on a hill and the greenery surrounding the home is lovely.

As we entered, we greeted Patrizia. We've only met her twice before as Maurizio is the one who handles any issues we encounter with the apartment. Patrizia's English ranks as limited, while Maurizio speaks very well. After a tour of their home, we sat in the living room. I looked and admired the photos in frames around the room and smiled at her. She introduced me to their family in the photographs and I placed my hand to my heart. She smiled understanding my sentiments.

The house stood larger than I expected, and the room was beautifully decorated. There were stunning views out each of the windows, and you could see far into the surrounding hills. I thought momentarily about what it would be like to live in a place like this. Gary would very much like to live in this type of home, rather than live in the city center.

Gary grew up in apartments and city life for the first half of his years. On the other hand, my upbringing encompassed the complete opposite. I grew up on Long Island in the suburbs. For me, walking out our apartment door and a few steps to a *café* is a life I never knew before. Running into people you know on the street and starting up a conversation lasting a half hour or more are experiences that I'm not familiar with. It's fun, spontaneous, and exciting to change plans and do something unexpected with friends you just happen to bump into. For now, I'm content with this city lifestyle. This doesn't mean I'll always want to live this way, but for now, I'm happy.

৺ A Special Travel Opportunity ৺

During one visit to Lucca, Lita and Guy informed us they wouldn't be in Paris but celebrating Christmas in the States. They invited us to come to stay in their Paris apartment where they've lived for years. It's not just any apartment, though. It's a stone's throw from the Eifel Tower with incredible views. It's always about location and theirs couldn't be any better. With all the travel restrictions, Gary and I went back and forth about it. *Should we? Shouldn't we?*

"It's an amazing opportunity," I said to Gary, and we began checking flights.

That's one of the best things about living in Europe. Most countries are relatively close and easily accessible. There are several airlines specializing in country hopping at very reasonable rates. We considered leaving the day after Christmas and returning before New Year's Eve. Both excited about the possibility, we started planning our itinerary... our very short, condensed version of an itinerary because of our brief stay.

Tickets booked, we watched the restrictions heighten due to the holiday. France increased its requirements for entry, even for us as Italian citizens. Italy also changed its mandates for reentry. *Oh boy.* This trip wasn't going to be easy.

A few days before we were to leave, I asked Gary, "Where are we going to obtain our COVID tests?"

Gary chimed in… "*How* are we going to accomplish this on Christmas Day? Nothing will be open."

We called the airlines, but they couldn't help us, and Ryan Air would not credit us to fly at another time. We stressed and tried to figure out a way. When we booked the airline tickets, we didn't think the entire trip through and anticipate any added restrictions. We were caught up in the excitement of going to Paris for the first time—and during Christmas, no less. What an amazing trip this would be, but at what cost?

Unhappy with ourselves for not thinking it through, we decided not to go. It just wasn't the right time. Another opportunity would arise, and we'd be better prepared. Perhaps at that point, travel restrictions would lighten up, and we'd have better opportunities to discover the beautiful country of France.

Winter Surprises

Bundling up for a walk around town, we head toward the *duomo*. Passing Piazza Napoleone, or Piazza Grande as locals call it, I tugged on Gary's coat jacket.

"Look, over there," while pointing with my other hand.

We see a large, outdoor ice-skating rink has emerged toward the south end of the piazza. We headed over to take a closer look. "Lucca on Ice" has taken over a quarter of this large piazza and roughly 197 by 98 feet. We stopped at one side, rested our arms on the wall of the rink, and watched.

Ice skaters were enjoying the fun, traveling in pretty much a counterclockwise rotation. A few younger, inexperienced skaters were holding on to a standing penguin providing them some stability while sliding across the ice.

"Can you believe this?" I said to Gary in amazement. "I never expected to see an outdoor rink in Lucca. What a fun and pleasant surprise."

We spotted a few lone adults in the center of the rink doing some spins while others hung on for dear life walking their hands, one over the next, along the perimeter wall of the rink. Most people sported royal blue ice skates indicating rentals. However, we noticed a few white pairs— worn by those who owned their own skates. This led me to believe that Lucca does this every year. We stayed quite a while, watching the skaters and enjoying the laughter—the laughter of those skating, as well as the chuckles from the crowd (including us) watching from safety. I pulled my scarf up higher under my chin and my hat lower on my head to cover my ears, it was time to go.

∽ Christmas ∼

Before we knew it Christmas had arrived, and we spent it with Gianna and Giacomo at their home. Pasquale, owner of one of our favorite restaurants, Osteria da Pasqualino Gubitosa, and a close friend of theirs, also attended. I oversaw the appetizers. To say I was a tiny bit intimidated cooking for Pasquale is an understatement. Despite that, he's such an easy-going person, I knew it wouldn't be a total disaster.

Giacomo suggested we initiate Pasquale in the fun American "White Elephant" gift game. We all agree on a reasonable euro limit for each gift. Gary and I started searching the stores along Via Fillungo for possible ideas.

"Both Giacomo and Pasquale own enough wine," I muttered to Gary, "we're not buying wine as a gift." Gary agreed. I continued, "I'd really would like something unusual, something different, but what?"

We searched for several days with nothing to show for our efforts. Finally, Gary and I decided on a good Lucca olive oil and a special box of chocolates. Not the grand gifts I wanted, but we should've begun our search earlier. We played the game up in the *altana,* tower room, and it was a lot of fun. Gary and I both chose wisely—and we all giggled that the two things Gary and I wanted to buy for ourselves, were the exact two things we both selected for our presents. How often does that happen? I wanted to purchase Amara, a Sicilian liqueur boasting a mild orange flavor for Dario's orange cake recipe given to me by Lita. She uses it to change up the recipe rather than always using Vin Santo.

The other item—new *Scopa* cards. The Italian pronunciation [sko-pa] literally means "broom." *Scopa* is an Italian card game, and one of two national card games primarily found in Italy, the other game is known as *Briscola.* Throughout Italy, you will see, especially men, sitting under a tree in nice weather playing this game. A crowd huddled around a table for four outside a bar or *café* is a good indication a card game's taking place. The Sicilian deck we bought in the States didn't have numbers printed on them. We liked Gianna and Giacomo's deck much better. Along with two new *Scopa* decks, a variety of *Toscane* and *Triestine,* a box of UNO cards also accompanied the gift bag. Such a deal! I'd never taken part in this game before and came out as such a winner. We realized, of course, that Gianna and Giacomo probably recalled us talking about both these items we wanted to purchase for ourselves at one time or another. They're so observant. It's just odd Gary and I both chose these exact wrapped items. I guess it was meant to be.

The day continued, filled with lots of fun, great wine, and food, all enjoyed with good friends. *What could be better?* Well, perhaps if spent with our grandchildren, but we knew this was a consequence—holidays will always be difficult living so far away from them.

Besides the White Elephant game, we received a very creative and thoughtful gift from Gianna and Giacomo. They are fortunate enough to own a car. They both know Gary and I don't like to impose asking them to take us to a store, especially IKEA in Pisa. When we first moved into the apartment, we seemingly needed everything. Let me rephrase that: it wasn't so much a matter of need, but we wanted our new apartment to be comfortable with several additional items. Grocery shopping on our bicycles is a different story. There's only so much shopping that can be carried out with this mode of transportation.

Their creative gift—a personalized card… but not just any kind of random greeting card. Their card included individual coupons creatively designed by Gianna on the computer: coupons for a trip to a medical appointment, a ride to the supermercato, a day trip to Chianti, to Brico, and of course, a ride to IKEA in Pisa. This was the perfect gift for us. Our gift to them?

They own a beautiful set of various-sized black and white patterned ceramic bowls and plates they bought in a local store in town. We happened to buy the same small bowls but in various colors and patterns. One of our small bowls turned out to be the exact black and white pattern they owned. Earlier in the year, one of their small bowls broke, and the store no longer carried the same pattern in the same size. I never made the connection, it just never clicked that we owned a bowl matching *their set*—their set, now one short. Gary and I both agreed we would wrap and bequeath our used bowl and give it to them to complete their set once again. They loved it.

The twist to this gift exchange among good friends? We both received something we could use and none of us paid a euro. All gifts of love and friendship and a moment greatly cherished.

☙

As the year came to a close, I'm reminded of how much I'm missing family. Nine months have passed since being physically together and although FaceTime is great, it sorely lacks the emotions I need as a mother and grandmother. Nana needed some lovin' and it weighed on me just a little bit more than I thought—or let on to others. Cards and gifts were sent, but it's not the same as picking out something with the older grandchildren or going shopping and experiencing them picking out things they'd like for Santa to bring them. Nonetheless, I must remind myself that we created this situation by moving abroad, and this choice came with consequences, as we all know. This one pulls a bit heavy though on my heartstrings.

Happy New Year

We rang in the New Year at Gianna and Giacomo's lovely apartment, with their extraordinary 360-degree views of Lucca from the *altana.* The evening consisted of delicious food, very nice wine, and several various board games. We enjoy changing up the scenario of teams with guys against girls or couple versus couple. The wine was flowing, as it usually does when the four of us are together.

Our friendship with Giacomo has become a bit of a dilemma for me. He has affected Gary's taste in wine—and our budget. Well, not really, but it puts a good dent in it. Giacomo's love for old wines has favorably altered Gary's palate. Ultimately, isn't life truly about enjoying the good things, especially at our age? I too benefit from this evolution of Gary's palate—*certo,* of course.

I thoroughly enjoy watching Giacomo open, with anticipation, a good bottle of wine. What I think I love the most about the experience—he has remarkable knowledge. He shares why he likes it, why it should taste a certain way, and perhaps what you also might expect to taste. I appreciate that he's so kind and generous to us, knowing our budgets are not in the same ballpark. The analogy is major league versus minor league. When Giacomo buys more wine than his refrigerators or storage can or should hold, he holds a private sale for Gary. We love him. End of story.

As the evening progressed and the midnight hour drew near, we were ready for the countdown to begin by heading up to the *altana.* Prosecco poured; we each took a position in front of one of the four windows in anticipation. Ten-nine-eight, the countdown started, and I found myself holding my breath. Earlier in the evening, the weather persisted in being a bit overcast and even drizzled, *Will we even see any celebrations I wondered to myself?* Three-two-one, the skies around Lucca began to illuminate with color. We all started with the *ahhs* and *oohs,* each with a different vantage point of the fireworks and the city.

"Look over here," Gianna exclaimed with her digital camera in her hand ready to capture the evening's festivities.

The skyline's filled with explosions of color in reds, greens, yellows, and blues. Some appeared low against the horizon so they must be home-style fireworks. In contrast, high in the sky, rockets were launched around the city with the familiar loud boom, followed by the explosion of color. A rhythm developed and they surrounded us with energy. We scurried from one window to another to view the city from a different direction. It almost seemed we were all dancing to a slow waltz. Gianna and Giacomo have the perfect, ideal view from their western window of San Frediano, the beautiful Romanesque-style church with large mosaics on its façade. This is always a favorite view of mine, but tonight it's spectacular. The Guinigi Tower dominates the southern view, and the dark sky is illuminated around these two Lucca treasures making our photographs and videos sensational. Off to the north, and easily spotted hanging out on the wall, are some young adults with their display of roman candles and firecrackers. We all giggle as we noticed the *polizia* were approaching them on the wall roadway. They probably didn't see them, but we sure did. We all began wondering if they'll scatter or stay put. The event went on for quite some time and I'm surprised it was not finished within a few moments. Unexpectedly, excitement builds as the sound of shooting rockets began right outside their window.

"Missiles are being launched," I said loudly, "Right from your parking lot in the palazzo!"

As we all scamper to the north window, we are amazed. The explosions are at our eye level since we're up in their tower. We're all impressed with the celebration of the New Year in Lucca. We shared celebratory kisses during the midnight moment, but it took about forty-five minutes before the noise and frenzy of the pyrotechnics died down. The year 2021 had come and gone and 2022 started spectacularly.

Medical in Italy

In January, we decided we'd better accept the fact that these old bodies need an inspection—like bringing your car in for a checkup. Except, it's overdue for us, something we've been putting off since arriving in Italy. We first made our appointments to see a recommended English-speaking dentist. She's found right outside Porta San Donato, easily accessible on our bicycles.

Not knowing what to expect, we set our sights low as our dentist back in Arizona had boasted a nice, traditional office. It's difficult to think about going to see someone else, especially after patronizing the same dentist for over twenty-eight years. I'm a bit of a chicken when it comes to dentists. A bad experience in my younger years left a bad taste in my mouth, so to speak.

I remember my mother used to pick me up from school and take me directly to my cleaning appointment in North Massapequa, New York. My appointment was also persistently scheduled at three o'clock. This time of day also coincided with the television game show, *The Dating Game.* I liked watching the show, but not on days I sat in the dentist's chair. It always came across to hurt a little bit more when the guy or girl didn't select the same person my dentist would've chosen. Being quite vocal in his opinion, and in my mind, he took it out on me. At least that's what the twelve-year-old in me thought at the time. It wasn't true but it's a lingering memory I keep of my encounters at the dentist's office. Not pleasant.

☙

Walking up the steps to the office, Gary, and I both are quite surprised. The office is immaculate and modern, and the office staff friendly. Gary and I took a seat and filled out our papers. While filling them out, two of our friends came walking in to make a future appointment. I guess the word has spread throughout the ex-pat community. Both of us are completely satisfied with our teeth cleaning by the dental hygienist, and the office in general. Impressed, we made our follow-up appointments.

☙

Gary

As we mentioned early in our story, Italy's medical system is ranked quite high. This fact's very reassuring to an aging senior citizen who has chosen to live in Italy. With our *Tessera Sanitaria* cards, most things are free and those you must pay for are a lot less expensive than in the United States. Another comforting factor to us. The problem… you must forget how you did things in the States and learn how this new system works. The good thing about medical care in Italy? It's not run for profit. Instead, it's all about you the patient and making sure you are well taken care of.

☙

When we arrived in Lucca, I noticed the sight in my left eye had been progressively getting worse. Of course, I needed to wait until I received my medical card before I could do anything about it. I asked our friends Gianna and Giacomo who've lived in Lucca for over a year now how the system works. They laid out for me a step-by-step plan of what I would need to do to go ahead using the system. My vision's challenged, it would be nice to see better. I live in, arguably, the most beautiful country in the world, and it would be a shame if I could not see the beauty all around me. So here are how things work in Italy. Hold on to your hats!

First, you contact your primary physician, by text message or telephone, and tell him/her what you need to be done. In my case—an appointment with an eye specialist. At this point, he wrote a script or referral that I picked up at his office. With the script in hand, I headed over to the pharmacy, where they will make an appointment with the doctor of my choice. We decided to use the same doctor our friend Giacomo used for his cataract surgery. He's also rated one of the best eye surgeons in Tuscany. Leaving the pharmacy, with my script and appointment in hand, I'll be seeing, (pun intended) the doctor in six weeks, at his first available open appointment.

On appointment day, Ilene and I rode our bicycles to the doctor's office outside the wall about fifteen minutes from our apartment. Arriving at his office, we noticed there was no check-in station, just some seats in a hallway where you wait until you are called. When his door opened, he came out and asked my name and appointment time. He reappeared in a few minutes and asked me to come into his office and examined both of my eyes. After the exam finished, he confirmed I would need cataract surgery and gave me a script for the operation.

Informing me I needed to pay his fee at EUR 120,00, I guess specialists are not covered by my *Tessera Sanitaria.* After paying him by credit card, we head back to the pharmacy, to make my next appointment for the hospital. I originally thought this appointment might be for the surgery, but instead, it's for the hospital to check his recommendation, obtain my medical information, and lastly, set the date for my surgery. I guess my Italian language lessons are starting to pay off since I understood most of what I'm told during my hospital visit. Leaving the hospital with a date for the surgery, February 18, two days before my birthday, I had an anxious feeling in my stomach. Now I would just need to wait six weeks for my surgical procedure.

As it turned out, all went well with the cataract surgery. It was different in the fact that I had not been awake during my previous cataract surgery in the States, yet I was fully awake here in Italy. The best part… it didn't cost anything additional, other than the initial fee of the specialist who was my surgeon.

☙

When we arrived in Italy, we each brought a one-year supply of our medications figuring we would return to the States for the holidays, and we could re-fill any prescriptions at that time. Because we decided to stay in Italy, we realized we would need to see our doctor for our prescription refills and our annual check-ups. Since neither of us met our chosen medical doctor, we figured this would be a good time to accomplish everything all at once. Ilene prepared a health history sheet for him in English, translated into Italian on the opposite side to make things easier. A recommendation from Gianna.

I texted him requesting our appointments, and he replied about an hour later recommending we come in on Friday to meet one another. Remember, I've messaged him for two scripts already, but haven't yet met him. Not knowing what to expect, we arrived at his office almost an hour before our appointment time. We're filled in by our friends on what to expect and how it worked at his office. Although there's a secretary on his floor, she's not there to check you in for your appointment. Her job is to tell you what door to sit in front of and wait for the doctor to come out and take you inside his office. She also will help you make appointments for the doctors on the floor, or you can pick up a prescription from her. That's the sum of her position.

Our doctor opened the door to his office, asked our names, and invited us to come in. He went over our medical histories and suggested we undergo blood and urine tests. For Ilene, he also suggested a mammogram and for me, a computed tomography (CT) scan since he wanted to check on my enlarged prostate. With prescriptions in hand, we say *arrivederci,* goodbye and head to the pharmacy, to make our next appointments. As we left his office, we looked at each other and I chuckled to Ilene.

"He looks like the doctor in the movie, "*Back to the Future—Doc Brown*."

All in all, it's a good first impression.

ଓ

When we showed the prescriptions, the pharmacist told us we must go to the CUP, Italian pronunciation [koop] to make our appointments. So, we headed to the CUP, situated in the old hospital. We waited our turn only to find out no appointments are necessary for blood and urine tests. You just show up and wait in line. Easy peasy. For my scan, I needed to wait two days… wow—only two days. We expected to wait at least a month or so. Ilene is told her mammogram would happen sometime in April since in Italy women only receive mammograms every two years, and her last one occurred in April 2020. She could expect a call sometime in April to set it up. *Funny thing?* They called her three days later and scheduled her appointment for the very next day. Go figure. We left the CUP and headed back home to digest what happened, and how the appointment system works in Italy. Like everything else, it's a Catch-22 scenario. Hoops, hoops, and more hoops to jump through. *Ahh, la dolce vita!* Long story made short, we learned, we accomplished, and all was well.

ଓ

Ilene

Our visit to the dermatologist, however, turned out a bit different than anything we experienced before. Again, with close proximity to the city center, we found, through a referral, an English-speaking young dermatologist. Gary has a history of skin cancer, and he needs to be examined on a routine basis. For me, my father always nursed issues with his skin, but he loved the sun.

I recall as a young girl while living in North Massapequa, my father would be outside soaking up the sun. Even with snow on the ground in winter, he'd shovel a small path for himself. Enough space for a folding chair next to the metal shed in our backyard. Here you'd find him sitting with his winter jacket on and a reflective trifold sunscreen in his hands basking in the sunshine. In hindsight, we know how harmful his routine was to his health and he eventually suffered from skin cancer. I'm not sure he fully realized the risks at the time. In those days, few made the connection between sun and skin cancer.

ꕥ

As we waited in the chairs outside the correct office door number, the young doctor appeared. I inquired if we should both come in at the same time. She said it was up to us. I shrugged my shoulders, and with an upturned hand, gestured for Gary to enter the office too. We sat down and briefly reviewed our health history. We presented her with our prescriptions from our medical doctor, but she said we didn't need them because she's a private doctor. *Ahh,* understood. We're becoming proficient in using this system. This also meant we would pay for this visit. If we went to a public doctor as part of our *Tessera Sanitaria*, there's a good chance it would be free. Note to self. It wasn't a big problem, and we figured a doctor in the system might not speak English. We decided to continue with our appointment. Gary went first.

As I sat and surveyed her office, it looked very different from what we were used to. The doctor's desk and chairs along with the examining table and a sink are all in one open room. No curtain in a corner or some private area. No paper robe to put on. *Nada.* Not even a nurse to act as a chaperone to protect her from possible false allegations of improper conduct by a patient. She simply told Gary to undress, and so he did… right in front of her desk. After his examination, it became my turn.

I'd already started taking off my shoes and socks toward the end of Gary's checkup. I paused and gasped to myself—I hadn't shaved my legs. *How could I have forgotten?* This would never have happened back in the States, I'd have been mortified. *Why was this appointment any different for me,* I wondered to myself. As Gary hopped down from the table, I mentioned it slightly giggling out of nerves or embarrassment to Gary and the doctor. Perhaps she won't notice—I doubt it.

With a clean bill of health for both of us, and because Gary has encountered some issues in the past, he's to return every year. While for me, three years unless something unusual appears or any other dermatological issues arise. We pay her by credit card and head for our bicycles.

ʗ

Just so you know, or perhaps you don't want to know, because of our tiny, phone booth of a shower, I've now created another use for the other porcelain item you find in European bathrooms—the bidet. It's now the convenient way I shave my legs. Others might have come to the same conclusion, but it's just not possible to bend down and accomplish this task in our shower. Next year's visit to the dermatologist will be a different story.

New Friends

From the end of January through March, our dance cards were filled. Almost every week we showed appointments on our calendar to meet people who've read our first book. It's unbelievable. It's surprising and very special to us. Jim, one of the administrators of our weekly English Monday group, began teasing us. He requested we stop being good ambassadors of Lucca because of all the visitors. He was kidding, of course. Most Mondays, we were introducing people either staying in Lucca for a brief time or just visiting for the day.

ʗ

In the middle of February, we met Ann and Terry, a great couple from our hometown in Phoenix, Arizona. We connected with them right away and started reminiscing about all the same places we all enjoyed, and all were completely baffled by how we never ran into each other when living there. Yet here we were, connected by a story Gary and I weren't sure anyone would want to read. Terry enjoys wine as much as, or even more so than Gary, so it became a unanimous discussion and beverage of choice at many of our dinners together. We enjoyed seeing the love of our "perfect Italian town" in their eyes. Through their excitement, I could see them living here.

Another surreal moment… as it turned out, they found an apartment and made an offer before leaving Lucca. Wow. We knew they fell in love with this town… and now their hearts found their home too?

☙

At one of our dinners at a favorite restaurant we've mentioned before, we noticed Pasquale speaking to a lady sitting alone at the next table. Pasquale was being very attentive as always, but possibly more so. Perhaps it was my imagination, but I began to wonder if she happened to be a celebrity. I'm intrigued. In my usual fashion, I introduced myself to her and the rest of our table. Martha was delightful and lovely. We found out that she's in Lucca for three months studying Italian. She's vacationed here several times over the years immersing herself in learning the Italian language. Her husband, Frank was due in Lucca in a few weeks to join her.

I mentioned our group, and invited her to the next English Monday. Over the next few weeks, we developed and enjoyed our new friendship. Its times like this I don't understand our daughter, Ally, or her significant other, Brett. They laugh and mock our gratification talking to people, as they are very happy keeping to themselves. When Frank arrived, we enjoyed his company too. They might hail from upstate New York, but they are fellow New Yorkers just the same. We enjoyed spending time together and know we'll continue to stay in touch. We were sad to say goodbye for now but know that we'll see them again one day in Lucca.

Lerici

Longing to do a bit of hiking and enjoy the outdoors, I inquired when Joanne from Florida has her next hiking adventure scheduled. She gave me the link to the group she's going with soon to Lerici, pronunciation [LEH-ree-chee]. Just a short distance south of the famous Cinque Terre, Lerici is nestled in the Gulf of Poets. Famous poets and writers claim this town inspired them by its beauty. It's a jumble of well-kept pastel buildings found along the crescent-shaped gulf covering high rocky cliffs, appearing to become one into the sparkling sea. This town is not as well known outside of Italy. Let me rephrase—it's not as "touristy" as most. When I see photographs on the Internet of the gorgeous promenade that follows the shape of the cove with small boats moored, I immediately wanted to go there.

Joanne hooked us up with a ride and we meet the group outside of Lerici in La Spezia. The group is comprised of Italian speakers, and I became a tad bit intimidated at first. My Italian's not good enough yet to carry on a conversation. This would be a true test for me. I haven't hiked in several years, but this ranks as one of Joanne's favorite towns, so I must see it for myself.

As we begin, I realized that I'm the only one without walking sticks. I murmured to myself, "*I hope it isn't an issue.*" With cars parked and secured, everyone walked up the hill through the town. The setting is quaint, and I spied a few residents gazing out their windows at the group of twenty or so of us marching down their itty-bitty walkways. Neighbors could probably pass butter and eggs to one another. Perhaps it wasn't the number of us, but the sound of all the walking sticks clattering on the cobblestones bringing them to their windows. Several of us stopped and took photos along the way. Far off in the distance, I saw the beautiful blue sea. Joanne and I stopped and took a few selfies with the beautiful backdrop. *Andiamo!* We were moving again.

The residents of this town must stay in good physical shape. The walkways are quite steep, and I'm hoping after several years of not hiking, my decision to come with Joanne was not a mistake. Still, I pushed on and try not to think too much about my thighs already talking to me.

After crossing a road, we entered a wooded area. The group in single file followed our hike leader, Guido. The path is clear, and we were following a stream. I heard the babbles or ripples of the creek, and the setting was simply breathtaking. It's quite relaxing just taking in the sounds of the moment. It reminded me of hiking through Oak Creek Canyon back in Sedona, Arizona—one of my favorite places to hike with the family. Leaves were scattered on the trail, and I stayed extremely careful with my foot placement, especially without any walking sticks to help my balance. I did, however, buy an inexpensive pair of hiking shoes with deep treads rather than using my everyday sneakers. A good purchase I thought to myself while lost in the silence of the forest around me.

As we emerged from the forest, we were on a paved street headed for what I assume might be another point to start our descent. We all stopped, took a break, and regrouped. At least I wasn't the last one the pack was waiting for. So far, it's a good sign. From this vantage point, I could spot Lerici down below and the castle dominating the town. This castle was built by the Pisans around the mid-200s.

I whispered to Joanne, "Are we going down to the water"?

She nodded her head in the affirmative and all I can think of...when we go down—we must come back up. Oh boy, fingers crossed I can make it.

From the sign I spotted, it looks like we've stopped in La Serra, a typical Ligurian village above Fiascherino beach in Lerici. Someone in the group pointed out that she knew the people living part-time in a house right in front of us. The home was beautiful, and I could imagine the joy of waking up every day to the views of the sea below. While we gathered our gear again, I noticed a small cruise ship or yacht anchored in the cove. It looked small from where we stood, but it would likely be larger than I thought. The sea was an extremely deep blue color and there was not a cloud in the sky. What a glorious day to be scampering through Italy.

We followed our guide off the paved street down another path toward the sea. Most everyone in the group knew one another from doing weekly hikes together through Tuscany. Joanne was relatively new to the group but knows some of the people already. I find only a handful in the group who understand and speak a little English. I tried to start a conversation in Italian with a few people using basic words I knew. I attempted to explain the beauty surrounding us and I think I was successful but not positive. I received a lot of smiles, so I don't know whether they appreciated the fact I tried or were just being polite. Either way, I'm proud of myself for attempting my newly acquired Italian. Still, when I found myself near Joanne, it was nice to chat in English for a bit, but I didn't want to monopolize her. I knew she was enjoying working on her Italian as well.

The path took us through backyards filled with olive trees and vines. Each yard appeared surrounded by fencing but the pathway looked picturesque. Guido stopped and began explaining something, and I could only understand a few words here and there. I'm pretty sure he's telling the group about the area. This is what I gathered from him holding out his arm, index finger pointed, and moving his arm slowly from left to right in front of him, in a horizontal spanning slow motion. He regained the head of the line and down, down, down the slope we descended until we reached the castle I spotted from up on the road.

Joanne and I stopped and took photos of each other in front of the Gulf of La Spezia and all the white fishing and sailboats moored neatly in lined rows. The seagulls kept dancing around us

dipping low, almost close enough for you to touch. There before us stood the Lerici Castle. I leaned back straining my neck to see the top. It's considered one of the most impressive and beautiful fortifications in all of Liguria. The irregular polygonal shape is surrounded by massive curtain walls in perfect condition. Today the castle is a museum and something I'll need to bring Gary back to see.

We were still descending, and steps take us down to the water level. Everyone's snapping photographs of the turquoise-colored water and camera-friendly shoreline. Finally, we reached the promenade. From here, we were told we can do our own thing for an hour, but we were to meet up on the other side of the crescent-shaped beach to continue the hike. Joanne and I decided to head right over to the opposite side of the cove. We walked along the cement promenade, shaded by tall trees on one side, and the sandy beach on the other. The views were spectacular. I stopped and snapped a few photos of the castle now behind us and off in the distance. People were laying and soaking up the sun on the beach, of course with their jackets and sweatshirts on. The sea remained empty of swimmers this time of year. Two of the most famous poets, Lord Byron and Percy Bysshe Shelley spent some time here in Lerici. I can see how these incredible surroundings aided their creativity.

When we all reunited in the piazza, I made the decision to wait for the group there, when they return from their added excursion. They were headed to Blue Bay, one of the most beautiful beaches in Lerici, and this part's quite steep. I just didn't want to push myself too far. They must come back through this piazza on the way back to the parking area. I know I must make it back to the starting point, and quickly determined sitting in the piazza, enjoying my lunch with a beautiful view would be a wise choice.

As they left, I searched my backpack for my sandwich. The aromas from nearby restaurants fill my senses and suddenly, my sandwich's no longer appealing. I headed for a seafood place and order a *frita misto di pesce,* fried seafood, to go. After enjoying most of it sitting on a bench, watching children kick around a soccer ball and ride bicycles in circles, I headed over to another area of the promenade and watched several sailboats racing. The wind had picked up a bit and it's a great day for them on the water. The boats are moving at a pretty good clip, and I could easily see the angle of the list from my vantage point.

With still no signs of the group, I indulged in gelato. After all, I've undoubtedly burned enough calories to enjoy both lunch items. I continued dreading the thought of hiking back, and it was weighing heavily on my mind. After a short time, I heard Joanne calling my name and the group returned. After a brief pause for them to catch their breaths, we headed back to the parking lot.

Returning on a different path, we halt at a sign. Guido explains about "*Sentiero delle Parole…Tra Fiume e Mare,*" The Path of Words… Between River and Sea. We've stumbled across a part of a cultural itinerary path that enhances the environmental and landscape heritage of Montemarcello-Magra-Vara Park. It's a route along the Magra River to the Ligurian Sea. Even in Italian, I could understand he's explaining the route and how you would continue in this direction while following the signs. Maybe I am truly making some progress.

As I spotted the parking lot ahead, I'm thankful. I released a sigh of relief and prayed no one was around to hear my loud audible breath. I prevailed and conquered—I did it. The hike totaled about eight and a half miles. I didn't complete the entire hike, but I persevered through most of it. Some parts of the journey became a little difficult with the ups and downs. Exhausted, I was looking forward to the drive back to Lucca. What a wonderful day to enjoy nature, and I thanked Joanne for inviting me. This group's too advanced for me in their hiking adventures, but they are a great group of people. There are lots of these groups throughout Tuscany.

Visits From Friends

March brought friends to Italy, friends we've never formally met. We've Zoomed several times, and of course, keep in touch by email and social media but to finally meet in person? We are excited. Gina and Jay are from New Orleans, Louisiana, and visiting Lucca for several days. Now being both from New York, I must say I giggle inside every time Gina says, "Y'all." It's a southern phrase that just doesn't roll off my tongue as a born and raised northerner. We've planned several things to do together, and we can't wait to show them, Lucca. They've rented the cutest Airbnb and it's close to the Guinigi Tower.

When we knew for sure they were coming to Lucca, the first thing we did was determine if we could acquire tickets to the *Carnevale di Viareggio*. After all, being from New Orleans, home of Mardi Gras, we knew they missed it this year in traveling to Italy. Why not take part in Mardi Gras... Italian style? The only day available was on their arrival to Lucca—the closing day. Oh boy… the craziest day to try and secure tickets.

The parade draws thousands of visitors of all ages who come to see the spectacular floats and costumes. We'd attended last year with Joel, but tickets had been sold out by the time we arrived, and we could only enjoy the floats from a distance down the streets. I was very disappointed that day not being able to join in the festivities, but this year would be different.

After asking for advice from several friends, I'm confident I could go online and figure out how to buy our tickets. Joel said he'd like to attend again this year, so I'm purchasing five tickets in total. After about a half-hour trying to decipher the different tickets available, I'm successful. The excitement had already begun building for me. All the photos and videos I've seen of past events were remarkable as the floats are huge, taller than buildings along the promenade. I emailed Gina that the plans are completed with tickets bought, and we're attending on closing day.

➳ Montecarlo ➳

Before our day in Viareggio, we arranged for the four of us to go on a private wine tour with some friends from English Monday. This group is so friendly and a valuable resource living here in Lucca. One great connection—Giovanni. He and his wife, Loreal are fun and truly nice people to hang out with. Giovanni provides transportation for tours and is a knowledgeable driver. Although this description doesn't define him well. They created The Tuscan Wanderer group together and will take you to almost any place you'd like to visit. He's a master at planning a custom trip based on what you might like to do.

Today, we were off to the small town of Montecarlo, about a half-hour drive from Lucca. After mentioning our excursion with Giovanni to others in the English Monday group, several people wanted to join us. We're thrilled, the more the merrier—especially when tasting wine. Gina, Jay, Gary, and I never journeyed to this famous town before, and we're looking forward to exploring it together.

The drive through the countryside was yet another amazing moment and suddenly Giovanni pulled over at the front gates of

Villa Torrigiani in Capannori. This town is about a fifteen-minute drive from Lucca. The Villa was stunning, and we jumped out of the van to take photos of each other in front of it. Gary and I couldn't pass up the opportunity to send the photo of us to our children with the subtitle, "There goes your inheritance, look what we bought." Of course, none of them believed us for a moment.

As we drove through the Tuscan countryside, the landscape was full of color and light. We are all quiet in the van just taking it all in. Arriving in Montecarlo, I wasn't aware of the town's size—it's tiny. We walked the streets as a group and met Giovanni out the other side of the porta. We're only stopping briefly on the way to the winery where we're planning to enjoy lunch. I mention to Gary that we need to return to explore more one day.

Arriving at our destination, the grounds of Fattoria Carmignani are pretty. It's a boutique winery and after a tour of the vineyard, we headed inside to the tasting room and lunch. The eight of us enjoyed fantastic food, wine, and conversation. We love finding out more about people. The food and wine pairings exceeded our expectations, and we would recommend this place in a heartbeat. After some purchases, we head back to Lucca but make one quick stop.

Giovanni turned down a dirt road and I think to myself, *where's he going?* Slowly he drove over river rock and navigated his way around some deep holes until he came to a stop. We all exited the van. We are standing in front of a huge oak tree. Giovanni tells us the story. This 600-year-old tree is located in the park of Villa Carrara and is known as the "Quercia di Pinocchio." It stands seventy-nine feet tall with a circumference of about fifteen feet. The unusual shape with branches almost growing horizontally reaches a diameter of 131 feet. It's phenomenal. In addition, we learn that beneath this tree the author of *The Adventures of Pinocchio*, Carlo Lorenzini (pen name Collodi) wrote several chapters of the story. This tree inspired him with the scene when Pinocchio meets the cat and fox under the oak tree. Later, the story goes, Pinocchio is hung by bandits who wanted to steal his gold coins but instead, the Blue Fairy rescued him.

This tree is also known as "The Oak of the Witches." One legend says the tree stood as a meeting point for witches performing their rituals by dancing on its branches causing the tree to acquire its unusual shape. Photos taken, we head back to Lucca and end another amazing day of life in Italy.

৵ Carnival of Viareggio ৵

The Carnival of Viareggio first occurred in 1873 featuring decorated carriages created by wealthy citizens protesting excessive taxation. It evolved into more of an event where ideas became expressed more freely and a bit of mocking the elite. The event has continued to grow and by the end of the nineteenth-century, the famous giant floats made their debut. Paper mâché was first introduced in 1930 and currently still used today. These beautiful and extremely complex floats take about a year to make. The creators are usually local artists, and a team builds these prodigious works of art in hangars at the edge of town. They are huge, quite thought-provoking, and inspired by international and Italian politics, as well as other current events. They are often represented in mockery forms. This event takes place over an entire month with five days of processions each year, one being on Fat Tuesday. Fat Tuesday's the well-known day of indulgence before fasting for six weeks of Lent. Did the 2022 event hold a big surprise in store for us to see and experience?

Arriving by train well before the start time of the event, we decided to grab some lunch. After showing them the beautiful marina and beach of Viareggio, we decided to indulge in some seafood. Agreeing on a restaurant, we each order our lunch. Finding our Frenchman friend, Jean, from Lucca enjoying lunch there too, we joined him. We run into friends everywhere. Jean wasn't in Viareggio for the Carnival event, but he happened to be in the mood for seafood that day. Each enjoying our lunch choices, we bid "farewell" to Jean and head to the entry gate.

Although there's a grandstand where you can reserve a seat, I chose to secure standing tickets so we could move around the experience. The first thing I noticed is "Burlamacco," the clown-like figure who's the official mascot of the Carnival of Viareggio. Burlamacco was created in the 1930s by painter, Uberto Bonetti. This clown character is all about not taking life too seriously, and encourages people to stay positive even when life is difficult. He's dressed in a bright white and red checked outfit representing summer with a long black cape and cocked red hat. He has his arms stretched out to the sky and stands on one foot. He starts every parade in Viareggio and so, with Burlamacco's presence, I know the event was ready to begin.

We find a relatively empty spot along the promenade, the street running parallel to the beach. The parade will start at Piazza Mazzini and head our way. Like other renowned carnivals in Italy, this event in Viareggio is characterized by visual displays of incredible artistry. My anticipation builds.

Music is blasting all around us. Children and adults are dressed in costumes, and many include painted faces. We each smile at one another pointing out special ones catching our eye. From up on one of the balconies, I spotted a woman dressed as Queen Elizabeth II in a light blue suit with a matching blue hat and a black handbag hanging on the crook of her elbow. She's standing next to a guy dressed as a Foot Guard for the Queen and waving to the crowd. He's in a red and white outfit with a large black bearskin hat holding a British flag. I prod Gary and point. He smiles as he sees them. The music's a bit loud, and it makes conversation difficult. We spend most of the time pointing and poking for the next few hours. Colorful paper confetti was being thrown by adults and children. There are bags sold at every vendor stall we see… and at that instant, the event began.

We spotted the first float approaching. There is a multitude of frolicking performers on foot in front of the float. They were wearing identical costumes complementing the float's color scheme and meaning. With their faces painted, they were dancing in a beautiful, choreographed manner. We were standing so close, that a few come near while I'm taking a video and startled me. Each of the allegorical floats plays its own musical soundtrack and are competing against each other in two separate categories—single and group floats. All winners will be proclaimed and announced tonight, the last day of Carnaval.

None of us acquired the event pamphlet, in Italian of course, when we first arrived. This brochure would've explained the various floats and their meaning. Some floats appeared easy to grasp, and you understood the symbolism right away. Two for me didn't need

any explanation. The first one, became the round COVID germ, a huge, spiky red and purple fuzz ball. This circular ball slowly opened like a flower, revealing a protruding menacing Chinaman's head with his tongue sticking out. His head shook back and forth—the meaning crystal clear.

Still, the political satire can even run sharper, in some years addressing scandals, gossip, or news stories. In the last fifty years, many floats have been eliminated, stricken by censure. Another one

I understood immediately—the one with Joe Biden riding a red and white striped bull with a blue head adorned with stars. We'd heard from other American friends in Italy about this float and waited with anticipation. President Biden was wearing an oversized cowboy hat. Although the funniest part of this float arose with the view of the four or five smaller Donald Trumps floating around the bull. I couldn't make out what each of them symbolized, but two Trumps held pistols. At the rear of the bull sat Vladimir Putin. He's holding the balls of the bull, decked out in red and white stripes. A political statement for sure.

My videos and photos were awesome as the floats passed right above me. I quickly realized some of the floats looked wider, forcing us to yield and shift back a bit from the promenade. We stood for several hours enjoying the floats and the festivities of the evening. Fading fast after the long warm day, it was an easy, unanimous decision to leave as none of us wanted to wait for the fireworks to begin.

☙

We headed back to the train station for our ride back to Lucca. Unfortunately, our return home wasn't without incident. The sidewalks in this town, like most in Italy, are narrow and uneven. When you add less streetlighting, it becomes dangerous. As we've mentioned to many people, you must look down while walking on cobblestones. You never know when one's missing or, shifted to a different level.

As we headed back, walking in the street became difficult with the traffic and number of cars because of the event. Gary and I prefer to walk in the street in this town because of the tiny sidewalks but somehow, we wound up heading back to the train station on the sidewalk at one point. There are remnants along this street of low, barely visible sidewalk planters. The trees are long gone but some of the uneven, slightly raised cement containers remain.

As we walked, Gary was located in front of me in a conversation with Jay. The next thing I knew, I watched in slow motion as Gary went down—straight down on his stomach. We all ran over to help him up and the first thing I saw on the ground was blood. My heart sank. Did he knock out a tooth or hurt his eye, which just underwent surgery? My mind was spinning. We all knelt around him and managed to sit him up on the small curb. After assessing, we discovered he had a cut on his forehead and his nose was a bit scratched up. However, it was his left hand—it had a huge, deep gash in it. I dug through my pocketbook, as did Gina, for some tissues, finding none. I looked up and saw a gelato store and Gina and I ran into it for some aid. I couldn't recall the word for napkin, so I try and convey to the employee what I needed by pointing to the small dispenser of napkins on the counter. He handed us a few and we ran off back to Gary.

A young woman, with her children and mother, stopped and asked if we needed any help. In my best Italian, I try to tell her I think we are all right. She mentioned there's a pharmacy, at the train station. We thanked her and they continued on their way. I'm very concerned. Gary's forehead doesn't look good, and we can't stop the bleeding on his hand either. After a few minutes, we know we must catch this train back to Lucca. We can't miss this one as the next one's about a forty-five-minute wait. When we stabilized Gary a bit, we headed for the pharmacy, and the station.

Walking into the pharmacy, the woman behind the counter saw Gary holding napkins on his forehead. I buy gauze for his hand, and she took him into a side room where they appear to do some clinical work. She sat Gary down and cleaned out the wound on his forehead and hand. With a bandage on his forehead and his hand wrapped up in the gauze, we thanked her, then headed for the platform in the station. For the entire ride home, I kept gazing over at Gary. There's blood on his jacket and shirt and not just a little bit. This was serious.

When the train arrived in Lucca, we took Gary directly home.

I mentioned to Gary, "Let's take a taxi home and arrive faster," but he insisted on walking.

We bid the others good night and once inside the apartment we tended to the cuts again. The cut on his hand was very deep, and Gary finally agrees to go to an emergency clinic. *But where?* We never investigated where we would need to go in case of an emergency like this. It was after eleven o'clock and we knew the pharmacy, was closed. I texted our friends Gianna and Giacomo and they promptly responded, recommending we take Gary to the hospital. I'm ready to go and Gary decided at the last minute it's not necessary. The bleeding had gotten under control, and it wasn't worth the walk to the hospital. I insisted we would call a taxi, there's no way we would walk. My heart sank but I accepted his wishes.

The adrenaline kept us up for a little bit, I'm sure. My main concern was his eye, and sure enough the next day, Gary began to turn purple around his surgery eye. I nagged him, urging him the entire next day about contacting the doctor to make certain he experienced no serious injury, just in case. Gary insisted he was fine—except for his pride. It took texting his daughter, Melanie who's a nurse to convince him he must see the doctor. His vision might be fine but who knows what kind of trauma could be happening behind the eye? Gary finally agreed and made the appointment.

☙

Carnaval turned out to be a memorable day and an experience I'd recommend to anyone being in Italy during this time of year. Several of our friends went to Venice and their photos of the costumes appeared over the top. Celebrated differently there, it's more about the elaborate costumes and people posing for photographs at the most beautiful, picturesque Venetian backdrops. All in all, a great day… except for Gary's mishap.

☙

Thank goodness in the end, Gary suffered no damage to the cataract surgery or his eyesight. The doctor did give Gary a prescription for some vitamin E tablets to aid in the healing process. Lesson learned, take your time walking the uneven streets and sidewalks in Italy. If you miss your train? There's certainly another.

Vintage Fiats

For the next big event with Gina and Jay, we sort of invited ourselves. We are not shy by any means. Gina told us they rented a vintage Fiat traveling the Tuscan countryside. *Say what?* When I mentioned it to Gary, he told me to find out more about it. Drive the Vintage is a rental company in Lucca and the company owns a fleet of vintage cars you can rent for the day. Gina and Jay welcomed us to join them. Cinquecento, as the company's website, describes:

> "An undeniable symbol of Italy. It represents the Italian style, the dolce vita, the 'daughter' of the economic miracle and, despite its age, its charm remains the same." *(Drive the Vintage, drivethevintage.com)*

☙

We walked outside the wall to their location. The owner, Luca explained the quirks of driving a car of the past. Gina and Jay chose the 1969 light tan Fiat while Gary and I took the 1965 red one. They both looked adorable each with an old piece of luggage strapped to the trunk. Once ready to roll, Luca and his friend climbed into the lead car. It's a light powder blue, 1965 Volkswagen Beetle. We could've used a map and driven unaccompanied, but Gina thought we'd all enjoy it more if we weren't concentrating on what road to take. After all, if you've driven in Italy, you know the streets are well marked... *Not.*

With our walkie-talkies on, we made our way out of Lucca to the countryside. Both of us enjoyed our sunroofs open and the weather couldn't be more glorious. Luca would use the walkie-talkies to advise us when a turn was approaching—*a destra,* right or *sinistra*, left. We traveled small, winding, breathtaking country roads. There were several old, abandoned stone buildings along the roadside, some with roofs caved in which added to the scenic charm. Tall thin cypress trees lined the roads while in other places olive trees prevailed. I took bunches of photos of the back of their car, as they're the lead dog, so to speak, while Gary's driving ours.

Luca's voice came on the transmitter, speaking in his best English, advising us to slow down as we were stopping ahead. As we pulled to the side of this single-lane road, Luca hopped out and took a photo of the four of us. Gina and Jay grabbed a kiss while Gary and I held our arms stretched out the window and the sunroof waving from our car stopped just behind them. It's the snapshot of the day. It's so perfect, it should appear on a billboard somewhere. A magical capture I will always remember and smile about.

While taking our time and leisurely following the winding road, Luca played Luciano Pavarotti singing "Nessun Dorma" from "Turandot" on the transmitter. It brought a huge smile to our faces, and I heard Gina say the music was a great touch. Gary loves Pavarotti and I glanced over at him. He was grinning from ear to ear. Driving a vintage Fiat while listening to Pavarotti. Incredible.

As we began to approach Montecarlo, we ascended higher and finally arrived at our lunch destination. Montecarlo is a little jewel in the heart of the province of Lucca. The small village sits on the hill of Cerruglio and dominates the surrounding plains. It's famous for the vast vineyards that fill the landscape, and for the production of its exquisite wines. The small streets and well-preserved city walls looked stunning.

"We'll need to return another day," I mentioned casually to Gary to explore this town further and investigate *The Fortezza di Montecarlo*, the fortress located there. Oddly enough, this hailed the same town we briefly stopped with Giovanni just days before.

Built-in phases from the twelfth-century up until the sixteenth-century, I paused to look around again. This town can't boast more than 300 residents living within its walls. It truly is tiny.

As I'm lost in the charm, Gary called to me as they've walked up further in the street toward our lunch spot.

We enjoyed a quick delicious lunch and back in the little Fiats we went—back to our starting point. We had a bit of a deadline for the return trip home, as we had encountered a problem with our water heater in the morning and our landlord made an appointment for a repairman to come later in the afternoon. We agreed to meet him at the apartment for the needed repairs.

Traveling a different way home, we passed under the Aqueduct of Nottolini, the beautiful Neoclassical style aqueduct stretching a little over one and three-quarter miles from near the city of Lucca to Pisa. The nineteenth-century structure brought water to Lucca from the mountains south of the city through a system supported by more than 400 beautiful arches. These arches are often confused as being from ancient Roman days, but the architect, Lorenzo Nottolini began construction of this major undertaking in 1823. So, not Roman at all. There's a beautiful hiking trail along this amazing structure called, *Via degli Acquedotti,* where you can walk or bicycle between Lucca and Pisa. This, too, gets added to our list of things to do. I captured a wonderful photo of Gina and Jay driving under the arches.

The day was absolute perfection. A leisurely drive through a piece of Tuscany in a vintage Fiat 500 with good food and friends. Another priceless moment living *la dolce vita.* It's something we've never done before but would certainly love to do again. I can easily see a large group of friends renting several of them and making a big, long procession line through the streets of Italy.

Life in Lucca After a Year

Ilene

My friendship with Joanne took on another surprise. Not only does she enjoy the outdoors, but I find out she used to be a yoga instructor in Florida. As she settled into her apartment, she decided to hold some classes for friends. At one time, I worked for a great pharmaceutical company that supplied its employees with free yoga and Pilates classes during lunchtime and after work hours. Yes, it's true. What floored me at the time, was that so few people took advantage of this extraordinary gift. My department was the largest in the company, and only two or three of us attended regularly. So, my yoga journey continued although it took my body some convincing it should twist and stretch the way it used to. I'm thinking too much pasta and vino are the culprits, but that's just my opinion. *It can't be that I'm older, right?*

☙ More New Friends ❧

We received an email from a couple coming to Lucca. Remember Margie, our chef, and farmer from Little Rock? We received an email from her cousin advising us that they're arriving in Italy and would like to meet. We planned to meet them at our favorite bar, Vinarkia on Via Fillungo.

Somehow, I mixed up the relationship and it wasn't Lynn who was Margie's cousin, but her husband Sam. It was so nice to chat and find out more about their life in California, and we were quite stunned to hear about the current high gas and food prices. We knew from talking with family in Arizona that costs had gone up, but not quite as much as in sunny California.

What turned out odd about the entire evening? Margie and I have enjoyed a friendship for quite a while taking online Italian lessons in the same class on mi.o. So, Margie and I go way back. However, Lynn and Sam never met Margie even though they are family. Sam met her when they were very young, but not as adults. When they return to the States, they've made plans to go to Arkansas and reunite. We can't wait to hear about this long-awaited reunion.

We spend quite a few days with these two and enjoy every moment. Dinner, *aperitivo*, and walking the town showing them Lucca. They especially enjoyed meeting our friends at English Monday. If someone visits us on a Monday, we often suggest we attend, even for a little while, for them to gain a feel of what other ex-pats think about life in Lucca. It's truly an amazing group of people.

ශ

Here's a perfect example of how small the world truly is. Reminiscing back to the first time we attended an English Monday meeting, Jim, one of the administrators of the group, introduced us to a few people. As we sat, we began talking to others at our table. A nice man, Bill introduced himself and asked where we were from. We told him Gary was originally from Queens, New York, and that I was born and raised on Long Island…

Bill interrupted and inquired, "Where on Long Island?"

"North Massapequa, in Nassau County," I replied.

Bill's grin slowly grew. As we drilled down deeper and deeper, we discovered we both graduated from the same high school, Plainedge. Bill is a few years older than I am, so clearly, we didn't graduate in the same class, but he started rattling off some names he thought I would recognize. I didn't but what are the chances we both meet in Italy—in Lucca? It's truly a small world.

ଔ

We've received the honor of being interviewed and featured before on a great site, MyBelPaese with Kim. It's a relocation network for Italy lovers, dreamers, and doers. Mike from Florida wanted to move to Italy and endured overwhelming questions with no answers. Kim's idea was that Gary and I might help Mike with information, and she would use it as a feature post on their site. We're happy to help Mike and Kim. Each email became more of a question-and-answer type format to help supply the answers to Mike's questions—meanwhile, his target date to move to Italy was fast approaching. He wanted to experience living here to see if it's what he wanted at this stage of his life. It's a great approach for anyone thinking of moving to Italy. Yes, it's the dream of some of us, but there can be quite a few difficulties living the good life in Italy. Quite a few.

With Mike finally in Italy, he emailed us he'd like to visit us in Lucca. We arranged the date and met him at the train station. I smiled as soon as I saw him with our book nestled under one arm. With hugs, we headed inside the wall to find a place to sit for *caffè.*

We find out more about Mike and his adventure. He has chosen the town of Certaldo, located between Florence and Volterra in Tuscany as his home base. He has visited this town before and loves it. He has already done some quick excursions through Tuscany since arriving.

We took the day to show Mike more of Lucca. The special sites and some not so well-known parts of the historic center. The weather's great, so we were not rushed at all. We arrived at our apartment and brought Mike inside. He, like everyone, loves our *terrazza,* terrace. It's the main reason we rented this place, we inform him. Although unusable in the very cold part of winter, we have bought a standing heater to help with chilly moments, and to use this outdoor space as much as possible—for as long as we can.

After choosing a place for lunch and order, I almost forgot to mention to him that Gary and I had just signed up to go with friends and Giovanni on a day trip to Certaldo and Volterra. If we'd known about the trip days before, we could've saved Mike a trip to Lucca to meet us. He informed us he was happy to visit Lucca anyway, but we will score another chance to meet in a few days when we visit his town.

We truly enjoyed meeting him and beginning a new friendship. After we bid farewell at the station, we promised to stay in touch.

~ Certaldo ~

Just a few days later, we met up with new friends Olga and Mariana from Florida as they also signed up for the day trip with Giovanni. We met these two amazing women as Olga read our book and the two came to stay in Lucca for a while. We enjoyed, and were fortunate to know, these two ladies better on several occasions during their stay. Several involved a glass of vino. I also think they both enjoyed meeting friends at our English Monday group.

Along with these two ladies, three other friends joined us for this excursion into Tuscany. With another glorious day, I'm eager to investigate a new town. I'd never heard or seen any photographs before about Certaldo. I wondered after meeting Mike why he chose this town. Visiting Certaldo would make ninety towns in Italy Gary and I have visited to date. I think we've seen our fair share. In fact, it's possible many Italians haven't traveled this extensively in Italy.

To make our list, a town must meet certain criteria. We must spend a significant amount of time in the town, whether it's lunch or a day excursion, we can't be just driving through the town. So today, we added two towns to our Tuscany region list, Certaldo, and our lunch stop, Mazzola. So, by the end of the day, ninety-two towns and fourteen out of twenty regions. Not bad, Gary.

As we wind through the small back countryside roads the fields are pretty much empty. The rows of raised brown dirt from recent plows are sure signs sunflowers were planted and waiting to burst above ground level and stretch toward the sun. Summer is spectacular in Tuscany with fields of *giallo,* yellow rows of these tall beauties standing in a perfect line. The season normally begins in June, but they fully emerge in all their glory in July. Their heads will begin to bow in late August when the season and the heat will bring an end to their summer show.

There's a lovely, fascinating legend about the sunflower. Clizia, a nymph, was in love with the Greek god of the sun, Apollo. Clizia followed him all day as Apollo rode his chariot through the sky. After Apollo rejected her, Clizia started crying in the middle of a field and didn't stop for nine days. She watched her beloved Apollo cross the sky while ignoring her. Apollo decided to transform her into a gold flower—the sunflower, that changes direction during the day, just as the sun moves in the sky.

As we approach, we observed Certaldo up high on the hill. Giovanni found his preferred parking lot and as soon as we exited the van, church bells began ringing harmonizing with our arrival. Standing directly in front of the church, they were quite loud, and we could hardly hear each other speak. Giovanni waved us to follow him to the funicular. We each paid our fare waiting for the car to come down from Certaldo Alto. As with many hilltop towns, there's a lower part of the city, usually more modern, and the medieval section, high on the elongated hill.

As we ascended, the views became more spectacular. We each held our phones and cameras ready and jockeyed for positions along the window area. Quickly arriving at the top, we disembarked and are transported back in time. Certaldo is a perfectly preserved medieval walled town abundant with quaintness and charm. I began snapping photos and we hadn't even arrived at the main street. We arranged ahead of time to meet Mike again, but this time in *his* town. As we all arrived at the first main street, I spotted Mike right away... he was the only one standing there, appearing like he was waiting for someone. Mike is tall, with a full head of white hair, a white beard, mustache, and a great smile. We exchanged hugs and handshakes, and I could tell he was happy we came to visit and explore his town. We introduced him to the group.

As we all walked the main street, my heart could instantly understand why Mike loves this town. The herringbone brick on the main street is in perfect condition and striking. I began taking photos of my obsession—doors. One after another, *snap-snap,* and the group had moved ahead of me. Gary and Mike were chatting with Giovanni while the rest of us were focused on this amazing medieval village.

I stopped and took a photo of an adorable red mailbox. It had put a smile on my face. The orangey-red stucco building had a hand-painted scene of a white dove carrying a letter in its beak. The bird was flying to the *posta* box where two other painted envelopes look like they are being dropped into the mailbox. A little bird sat on a nearby perch just watching the dove deliver the mail. It was creative and cute as a button. I finished taking about a dozen photos and noticed Mike's now standing next to me—shoulder to shoulder. I glanced over at him and told him I loved the scene painted on the building and confessed mailboxes are a thing for me too. I looked at Mike and he was grinning like a Cheshire cat.

"You're looking at my apartment," he said, "isn't it beautiful?"

We both nodded and continued standing there, taking in the beauty of this creative idea before continuing to catch up with the others.

Straight ahead stood the Palazzo Pretorio or Priori Palace, the seat of the government and court of justice. The magnificent façades were covered with terracotta coats of arms. Underneath a covered area in the front are beautiful, frescoed remnants and you can still make out some of the animals and symbols. They are old and worn but again, recognizable.

As we meandered down a small street, we stopped at a landing and an amazing vantage point. We gathered while Mike took a photo of the group with the towers of San Gimignano in the background. The maze of tiny streets continued to flow and I was capturing every door in town. Most of the homes here are built with brick with very little stucco noticeable. As we passed through several portas, Mike suggested we take a road outside the wall to acquire a great view of the castle. We didn't schedule enough time to go inside and explore, but it's the major presence in this village.

We learned a scholar of classic literature, Boccaccio, made Certaldo his home in his later years of life. His main work, the "Decameron," is still considered a pillar of Italian literature. He stood a great fan of Dante.

As the group walked down a paved Tuscan cypress-lined street, the panoramic views were breathtaking. Miles and miles of vineyards scattered the horizon. From this viewpoint, the striped rows of vines alternating between light and dark green were eye-catching. Stone houses with red clay roofs dotted the countryside. Mariana pointed out a few deer in the vineyard below hurdling over the rows of vines. By the time I unlocked my smartphone, they had disappeared and were out of sight. We all snapped a few photos of the castle and headed back to the funicular. We bid Mike farewell and told him to keep in touch. His town is special, and I truly understand why it captured his heart years ago.

Back in the van, we were stopping for lunch before arriving in Volterra. When I say the town of Mazzola is small, it's entirely possible we patronized the only restaurant in the town. An older gentleman walked near where Giovanni stopped to park, and we all began to giggle. The man was wearing a baseball-type hat with the town name, "Mazzola" embroidered on it. The volume of laughter slightly rose when someone in the group suggested he might have worn the hat to remember what town he's from—in case he gets lost. Perhaps it's one of those moments where you just had to be there, but it remained quite funny at the time. Poor guy… chuckling at his expense, shame on us.

Volterra

Although it was the end of March, the countryside was still quite bare. Nothing had begun to bloom and the rolling hills of Tuscany ranged in various shades of green and brown. Large groups of greyish-white sheep were easily spotted on the gentle slopes of the valleys. The naked vines in all the vineyards are a contrast to what we'll see in a few months. They'll change into lush vines with green leaves and bundles of white and red grapes hanging beneath them. At any rate, it was still early in the year. Twisting through the small streets, we can view Volterra up high on the mountain. Gary and I explored this amazing town twice before, and it's still one of our favorite Tuscan hilltowns.

Arriving, Giovanni pulled over to park in the piazza. As we exited the van, there are many motorcycles parked around the roundabout. I threw my hand out in a gesture to the group. Not like they would miss seeing all these Harleys, Hondas, and Yamahas, but I mentioned their ride through the breathtaking scenery and up the mountain must've orchestrated a spectacular encounter. Everyone shook their head and agreed. Gary and I started telling Giovanni about our Harleys we rode for a period back in Arizona. I think Giovanni might have been shocked at me owning and riding my own bike. I took out my phone and showed him a photo. Gary, of course, always mentions my pearl white Sportster 1200 Low with matching hard saddlebags, and that it looked like a police motorcycle. No police sported a wide black band with orange pinstripes, but I understand his reference. It never sat well with me, but I loved my Harley just the same.

Taking in the expansive views at this porta, we gathered and begin meandering through the streets as a group. Volterra is renowned for its unusual layout reminding us of its Etruscan origins. Strolling through the historic center, it's like stepping back in time. The buildings and cobblestone streets are well preserved.

One by one, several of us stand a bit taller and look around. *Do we hear drums? Where is it coming from?* Walking a bit further, we viewed an opening to the street below and find the answer to our unspoken question. A medieval parade is slowly passing, and we all decide to descend the steps to obtain a better view. At street level, we lined up behind others already gathered and jockeyed for a better viewpoint. Flag throwers, men carrying English longbows over their shoulders, and maidens in medieval gowns carrying flowers, all pass us in slow strides following the beat of the drums. The beginning of the procession was long past us and it was at that moment we determined the possible reason for the event. A new cardinal was visiting the region.

He was wearing his crimson wool cassock, white apron tunic, manteletta (short shoulder cape), and skullcap called a zucchetto—the crown-like biretta. The skullcap is the only thing a cardinal receives from the pope during his ceremony. Cardinals are associated with red because it's a papal color. He's surrounded by other priests, in their black and white cassocks and vestments, and perhaps the mayor of Volterra. I think it's a good guess as he's wearing a finely crafted navy-blue suit and tie with an Italian tricolor ribbon across his chest, embellished with a coat of arms embroidered on it.

After they pass, we had an unobstructed view of the street. I glanced up and over to Gary and smiled. He recognized the gesture and knew exactly what I was thinking. On the one half of the street, appeared dozens of beautiful flags displayed from buildings in a pattern of yellow and orange. The buildings in the other direction exhibited flags in the colors red and white. Yes, we were standing at the dividing line between two different neighborhoods or quarters, resembling other towns like Siena, Arezzo, and Foligno. Each neighborhood has its own colors, symbols, and flags.

Giovanni guided us to the Roman Theater dating to the end of the first-century B.C. When Gary and I stayed in Volterra, we passed this site each time we went to the parking lot. It was amazing to see it again. It's built in a natural amphitheater half-circle shape with many of the columns and ruins still standing. We all snapped photos and move on further down the street.

We headed down a small street and Giovanni finds the shop he wanted to show us was chiuso, closed. I wasn't aware Volterra's famous worldwide for its alabaster. Yes, it was that time of day when stores close for *riposo,* or siesta. Most people presume storeowners close to take a nap—but this is not the case. Well, perhaps in a few cases, but generally, most stores stay open late, and owners use this time to go home and eat lunch with their families, especially school-age children. This time is generally between one-thirty and three-thirty in the afternoon. It can vary but in much larger cities, some proprietors and larger department-like stores don't follow this practice.

As we began to head back, we arrived in Volterra's main square, Piazza dei Priori. This piazza's very large, and it's here you can appreciate the beauty of the thirteenth-century Palazzo dei Priori, the oldest town hall in Tuscany. The tower, destroyed during an earthquake had been rebuilt in the 1800s. It's also affectionately known as the Torre del Porcellino, or Tower of the Piglet, because of the small stone form of a wild boar you find at the top.

We found a stage toward one end of the piazza and a large gathering of people. Announcements are being made and with my small understanding of Italian, I can't understand what's being verbalized. I do, however, notice the cardinal and the mayor standing at the podium. As I glanced around and looked up, residents are watching, elbows leaning on open windows sills above. So as not to disturb the speech, we stopped and waited for a break in the action before heading around to the front side of the stage.

Drums and horns began to play, and I saw a group of flag throwers march to the open area in front of the stage. I know what's coming and I make my way closer to them. The wind was substantial, and I know they were going to experience difficulty catching the flags after they are strategically thrown into the air. Perhaps they already had a plan in place and won't toss them quite as high as usual. I love these medieval traditions. Traditions speak to my heart and Lucca has quite a few that have been practiced since medieval times.

The van became eerily quiet on the return to Lucca. A pleasant full day filled with beauty, good food, and medieval fanfare, all enjoyed with the company of new and old friends. These trips are special, especially when you don't own a car. Gary and I pretty much travel around using our preferred method in Italy—the train. Still, many of these towns are not accessible, and it makes days like this one exceptional. We try and choose these excursions, the ones we can't easily reach ourselves, for day trips such as this.

৺ A Moment of Reflection ∾

As the first of April arrives once again—as it does each year, Gary and I took a moment to reflect. We've lived in Lucca for one year. An entire year in one location. Well, two different apartments but in one town. Are we happy with our choice? Have our hearts found their home? You betcha. Lucca has become so special to us, in so many ways. Will we stay here forever? That's something my crystal ball can't answer—not currently. We know we feel comfortable here in Italy, especially in Lucca.

Gary always says, "He's American by birth, Italian by choice." It couldn't be truer.

ꝏ

For the most part, we love our rustic apartment. It's how I refer to it anyway. It's not perfect. I wish it featured a more modern kitchen and bathroom. I truly hoped for two bedrooms and two baths. Most of the time, I like my neighbors. Once upon a time, our bedroom existed as part of our neighbor's apartment. According to our landlord, the palazzo changes every fifty years or so. I assume he means it gets rearranged. We noticed a problem with our servant quarters—yes, that's what it amounted to at one time. When they closed and filled in the doorway to the neighbors creating our bedroom, they neglected the consideration of insulation. Therefore, when the couple next door has a conversation or throws a party—it sounds as though they're physically in our bedroom. I often think I should ask, *Can I offer anyone anything to drink?*

One Saturday night while they were hosting a party, Gary and I started giggling in bed. A guest next door started singing Billy Joel's, "Piano Man," and soon several joined in. It lasted only a minute or so but the fact they were singing in English made us both laugh. The fact they were also singing at one-thirty in the morning also made us put pillows over our heads. Oh, the joys of apartment living. Gary quickly took the opportunity to remind me this is the style of living I wanted. *I know Gary... but not now, not at this hour in the morning.*

As a bonus, there are times our neighbor practices the piano. If you stand in our living room or bedroom, you will swear his piano is in our apartment. At different times of the day, he practices. Morning, noon, and sometimes too late at night for me. At least he plays very well, and we like his choices in music. I'll grudgingly concede this fact, and I think Gary would agree.

He plays my favorite piece, "Clair de Lune" composed by Claude Debussy. I can close my eyes and easily visualize and hear my mother, Mazie, playing as I arrived home from grade school. Sometimes I would sit on the porch and listen to her practice before opening the screen door and announcing my presence home. Soon after moving into our apartment, Maurizio our neighbor began playing this piece. Gary heard it first and called me into the bedroom. I remember sitting on our bed, just listening—sobbing. Loving memories were brought back to me with just the sound of a few notes.

Hands down, our favorite spot in the apartment is our 340-square-foot *terrazza.* It's one of the nicest we've seen in town. It has a short wall around the perimeter and wide terracotta polished brick tiles. This short wall and the two walls of the apartment building itself are painted a cheerful creamy yellow to tie it all together. It came with a six-person table and umbrella. We've added a plastic wicker look-alike lounge set with a love seat and two chairs. It also has a cement sink and spigot making it convenient to water the plants.

Our terrace also features a small barbeque Gary insisted on buying. Another favorite item was a gift from Ally and Brett—an Ooni pizza oven. Oh yes, we've made some amazing pizzas and calzones in this oven already. When the weather became chilly, we bought a standing propane heater to take the chill off of the evening air. What brings this terrace to life, though, are the beautiful flowers and plants. A Sicilian lemon tree, flowering succulents, a small sago palm tree, one variegated rose bush boasting yellow orange-red blooms, a purple and white hydrangea plant, red geraniums, and calla lilies, now call this terrace home with the original three small olive trees which already existed here. Five small narrow pots line the perimeter shelf of the wall with the repetition of dark purple and white petunias. The herb section currently has thyme, parsley, oregano, rosemary, and basil doing well in the *sole,* sun. Arugula and three tomato plants are new additions and hopefully will soon supply some produce. We love this space and it's the main reason for renting the apartment. Our friends enjoy it as well, especially in the evening with the string of solar party lights illuminated and candles strategically placed all around.

Many days and evenings are enjoyed on this terrace. Gary and I love enjoying an *aperitivo* with a glass of vino or after-dinner drink. I especially enjoy watching and listening to the Swifts. They are among the fastest-flying birds in the world. They are larger than Swallows with long curving wings, which make them resemble a boomerang when soaring through the air. Their acrobatic maneuvers are simply captivating. They swirl and spiral almost flying in unison to a musical symphony. We easily spot them in groups maneuvering over the rooftops together. I've read they never land on the ground and almost their entire lives are spent in flight, feeding on flying insects, and even mating. Perhaps too much information? Still, it's fun to watch their never-ending dance while listening to them call each other emitting a high-pitched scream. Even the seagulls are enjoyable to watch how they fly and stay together in groups. We've heard owls, quail, and spotted tiny hummingbirds which are not hummingbirds at all—but small Italian moths. I love listening and watching all of them from our terrace—all but Bianca. Our annoying white pigeon who just won't pack her bags and find another place to live. How do I convince her this isn't *her* home?

☙

Although, it wasn't always this beautiful. When we first moved into the apartment back in July, the area visible from our terrace resembled piles of dirt and very tall weeds. Our landlord mentioned an Australian couple bought the property and work would soon begin. This couple also purchased the first-floor apartment in our building and the stone and brick palazzo which extends to its own building, next to this weeded area.

The entire summer stayed excruciating with windows open and construction noise beginning at eight o'clock in the morning. We would hear the clanking of the motorized gate and know the crew arrived. No possibility of sleeping in late, except on Sundays. The amount of dirt rising from the ashes in high plumes became mind-boggling. We dusted and cleaned almost every day—even the terrace. Constantly wiping things down became brutal. At one time we heard the distinctive sound of a weedwacker. At the end of the day, Gary and I came out on the terrace to see the damage. Yes, more dirt needed cleaning, but we both stood at the edge of the terrace with our mouths open in amazement. The wall on the side, originally covered in overgrown ivy and trailing plants became exposed. With the weeds gone, the wall transformed into a stunning white stone and brick backdrop—it appeared out of nowhere.

"Who knew it was even there?" we both unconsciously remarked at the same time.

Both turning to each other in disbelief, we shrugged our shoulders in bewilderment.

It took about six months for their backyard transformation. Our landlord stopped over one day to view their progress and told us the three ancient olive trees they just planted probably cost around EUR 40,000. I could not hide the shocked look on my face.

Maurizio has a great sense of humor. He looked at us and casually advised, "It's going to be beautiful, but I no charge you more."

After a long burst of laughter, Gary replied, *"Grazie Mille."* We're lucky in the landlord department as both he and his wife are simply wonderful.

A few times we were caught admiring this beautiful backyard. We also enjoyed meeting the new neighbors… well, if you could call it a meeting, speaking down to them directly from our terrace. They give the impression of being very friendly, and Joanne was even kind enough to apologize for the noise and dirt. As much as I appreciated her compassion and acknowledging the issue, there wasn't anything she could do about it. The bottom line? We knew it wouldn't last forever. They did a superb job in the design and execution of this wonderland we enjoy and admire from a distance.

A Reunion

Barbara, a very special friend, arrived at the end of March. We met her and her husband, Tom when we stayed two months in

Verona during our year adventure. Again, one of those chance meetings in Italy that's blossomed into an amazing friendship. I treasure this friendship. It's special to me, as are many we've made along this journey. We've mentioned them before and how we spent a week in Estes Park, Colorado with four of their friends after we returned from Italy that year. We met them again in Florence last year, and now Barbara would be in Lucca to study Italian for a month. Tom would join her for the last week. We are the luckiest couple in the world to meet such amazing people. Whether it's because of our book or blog—we find it incredible and we feel truly feel blessed in our lives.

It was wonderful to see her again and we caught up at our favorite bar, Vinarkia. We introduced her to Rebecca and Nicola, and she instantly saw why we love this place and bring everyone here. It's our *Cheers*. These two young Italians, who opened the bar just when COVID hit, are so warm and friendly. Their bar has an old-fashioned charm to it from the classy wood décor to the music selections. Cocktails are their specialty, but Nicola is very knowledgeable about wine, and they both truly know how to make their customers feel welcome. Gianna and Giacomo introduced us to them back in May 2021 when we first met, and we'll be forever grateful.

We spent a few hours catching up with Barbara at Vinarkia and know she was tired from her trip. Good thing she's staying in a bed and breakfast right across the street. It was wonderful to see her again.

We met Barbara, and enjoyed her company, quite a few times while she stayed in Lucca. Although, in between her daily classes in school, we most certainly didn't socialize as much as we'd hoped. Family also visited us for a week during this time which limited our availability. We introduced Barbara and Tom to Gianna and Giacomo who instantly became friends too. Friends meeting friends. Life's good in Lucca. As always, it's hard to see friends leave.

᯽ Family Visits Lucca ᯽

Gary

During a phone conversation with our daughter, Ally, and Brett, we learned they'd be on a business trip in the United Kingdom in April, and would like to come to Lucca and spend four days with us before flying back home to Las Vegas. Of course, we both were excited and we asked if there was something special they'd like to do, or a particular food they'd like to eat so we could start planning for their visit.

It took all of two seconds for Brett to say, "Pizza and plenty of it." This man loves his pizza! I truly believe he could eat pizza every day when he's in Italy. If my memory serves me right, when they visited us in Florence in 2019, he did enjoy a pizza just about every day.

Later in the week Ilene, and I started planning for their visit. Mind you, they weren't arriving for another four months, giving us plenty of time to plan. We decided to show them our town first, the Lucca we both love... and we hoped they'd love it too. Of course, it would entail plenty of walking and sightseeing. Views from the wall remain one of the best ways to introduce someone to Lucca. We decided to rent a four-seater rickshaw bicycle and enjoy some fun. To Ilene, you know just viewing and exploring Lucca would not be a complete vacation, something special would need to be included. The dialogue began on exactly what the special excursion should look like.

Since we helped Ally file for her Italian citizenship back in 2020, we hoped by the time they arrived in Italy she'd have received a letter from the Italian Consulate saying she was approved as an Italian citizen. We imagined how wonderful it would be to take them to Sicily and the town of Licodia Eubea where she too would register and pick up her Italian birth certificate as we did back in 2019. Since April was four months away, we put the trip on the list of possibilities but if she did not hear from the Consulate by then, we'd have to look at other places to go. We started discussing options. As luck would have it, she never heard from the Consulate in time for the planned April trip. Not surprising as the Los Angeles Consulate is notoriously slow, just as we experienced waiting for our citizenship. I guess some things never change.

ᗰ

As April grew nearer, we still had not come up with an itinerary we both liked. One night while watching television, I came up with a great idea. Of course, this change meant reworking the itinerary, but it involved doing something Brett loves to do—eat.

Excitedly, I looked at Ilene and said, "How about going to see Dario Cecchini and eat at his restaurant in Panzano in Chianti?"

The fact I wanted to change the much haggled-over itinerary did not sit well at first, but after a few moments of her considering the possibilities, suddenly Ilene smiled and said it would be perfect. The trip to Panzano became a permanent itinerary item and one of the special excursions we would take. We only hoped both Ally and Brett would like our choices.

Of course, we also wanted to make sure they both agreed with our plans, after all, it's their vacation. Happily, both Ally and Brett decided a trip to Panzano would be an excellent idea. So, why Panzano you might ask? Well, both Ilene and I thought they'd enjoy lunch at Dario Cecchini's restaurant and meet the man, the legend, himself… Dario. As an added benefit, I'd enjoy the opportunity to meet him too. If you've never heard of Dario, don't feel too bad. Both Ilene and I never heard of him either until Ally and Brett told us about a television show called, *Somebody Feed Phil,* on Netflix. The creator of *Everybody Loves Raymond,* Phil Rosenthal, travels the globe to taste the local cuisine. To make a long story short, he's a very funny guy, and one of the places he stopped during an episode—was Dario's. We later learned several Netflix specials and cooking shows featured Dario. After watching, we were hooked and became huge Dario fans, too.

Dario and I share one thing—we are both butchers. Well, years ago, when I was younger, I'd been one too. Me though—not so famous. That's one reason why I wanted to meet Dario. To enjoy some excellent beef and of course some Chianti wine too.

☙

We also decided to take them to the Cinque Terre for a day trip. Indulge in lunch in our favorite town of Vernazza. We learned of a fabulous seafood restaurant overlooking the sea from our friend and driver, Giovanni, and decided to make reservations. Ally and Brett both love seafood, so we were confident this would be another special day trip. After all, man does not live by pizza alone.

☙

Before we knew it April had arrived, along with Ally and Brett's arrival in Italy. We thought we'd surprise them and go to the airport with our driver. I planned to hold a name sign you see the limo drivers use just for a laugh but somehow, they knew we'd be at the airport to meet them. So much for surprises. As they walked through the arrival doors, I could see Ilene starting to tear up, and truth be told, so did I. We enjoyed their visit in Florence, but this trip was very special to Ilene and me. They're coming to see us where we now live, at our home in our beloved Lucca.

☙

We arrived at our apartment and gave them some time to arrange their baggage and things in our bedroom. Ilene and I decided we would sleep in the living room, giving our bedroom to them. The IKEA sofa bed would be comfortable for a few nights and would suit us just fine. Besides, they live out of suitcases, and better for them to use the bedroom instead of tripping over clutter and suitcases in the living room.

Since they appeared hungry, I made a quick sauce and threw it over some cavatelli for a light lunch. Shortly after, we rented a rickshaw in Piazza Santa Maria to tour the wall. I'm sure we were a sight to behold as we struggled to peddle up the ramp to reach the top of the wall, but once there, it was smooth sailing or should I say peddling. The wall is approximately two and a half miles around and you can enjoy the beauty of Lucca from the top of the wall. We made a few stops along the way to point out several special sights, including some of the history of Lucca. I think I must've told them my favorite fact about Lucca more than once. The fact the powerful Medici family from Florence never conquered Lucca—although they tried several times to no avail.

As usual, Ilene gave me a look and said, "Yes Gary... We know how much you love the fact about the Medici's failures with Lucca."

It just gives me a warm fuzzy feeling knowing they failed several times.

We finished our tour and walked through the city for a while before heading back to our apartment to enjoy pizza for dinner made in our new OONI pizza oven. A Christmas gift from them, they're anxious to see how good we're getting at using it. We also invited our dear friends Gianna and Giacomo over to meet the kids. I believe everyone enjoyed the pizza as well as the conversation. The following day our schedule involved our special excursion to our favorite town in the Cinque Terre, Vernazza, and introducing them to this wonderful part of Italy—Liguria.

Cinque Terre

Thursday, we caught the 10:42 AM train to Riomaggiore, about a two-hour trip from Lucca. The itinerary entailed taking in the sights in Riomaggiore, then catching the train to Vernazza for a two o'clock lunch reservation at Ristorante Belforte. It's a fantastic restaurant built into the cliffs overlooking the Mediterranean Sea. Ilene asked Giovanni if he would mind making the reservations so there wouldn't be any confusion with the language barrier. He was more than happy to oblige. Plus, this restaurant had been his recommendation, so Ilene assumed he might command some extra pull for a great table. Vernazza is one of our favorites of the five small towns in Cinque Terre. It has a natural amphitheater-shaped pier and is, perhaps, the most photographed village of these five little towns.

Unfortunately, the train arrived late in La Spezia causing us to miss the train to Riomaggiore. We didn't want to waste thirty minutes waiting for another train, and at this point, stopping first in Riomaggiore might make us late for our lunch reservations. On the spur of the moment, we decided to just continue to Vernazza and spend some time there sightseeing before lunch. There was only one problem with this plan… our tickets were for Riomaggiore, not Vernazza and without even thinking about it we just decided to stay on the train exiting at Vernazza.

☙

At this point, I need to tell you about a game Ilene and I play when we travel by train. We each predict whether or not the train conductor will check tickets or not before the train pulls out of the station. Although we always carry tickets for each trip, we just like to play the game. I sat down one day and figured we could've saved over EUR 1,000 by not buying tickets because the conductor never checked, but as I said, it's just a game we play.

☙

On this trip, we both guessed no one would check tickets even though we always carry them—or so we thought. In hindsight, we should've bought tickets from La Spezia to Vernazza but didn't even think about it. Exiting the train, we started heading for the stairway down to the town. There was a very large tour group also exiting, so we kind of blended in with the group. At the end of the platform, a Trenitalia employee was checking to see the group's tour passes.

Since we were not part of the tour, we continued walking toward the steps. From out of nowhere we heard someone yelling at us to show our tour passes. We calmly explained we were not part of the group and thought our answer would suffice. He firmly raised his one arm, barely stopping his hand before reaching my chest, and told us to *s-t-o-p!* His face appeared hardened and insisted to see our tickets. Without even giving it a second thought Ilene dug through her pocketbook and presented him with all our tickets for the entire trip from Lucca—asking if there existed a problem. He grabbed the tickets from her hand, going through them slowly, one by one. Looking them over, he said our tickets weren't valid for Vernazza.

That's when it dawned on us that our tickets were purchased for the town of Riomaggiore, not Vernazza. Ilene and I quickly glared at each other with wide eyes as we realized what happened. We tried to explain the honest mistake and that we'd gladly pay the fare difference, but he wanted no part of our explanation. He insisted that we were trying to beat Trenitalia out of EUR 20,00 and now we'd also need to pay a fine of EUR 50,00 each. For what appeared to be an eternity, we tried to apologize for our mistake, but he just kept talking over us, as his voice got louder and louder, repeating the charge—that we were trying to beat Trenitalia out of money.

Ilene offered a compromise saying, "We'll board a train to Riomaggiore and return to Vernazza later."

His face remained unsympathetic with his eyebrows furrowed and lips tightly pursed. "No, you pay the fine" he insisted.

By that point, we were all fed up with his arrogance and attitude as his yelling was causing an ugly scene. Brett stepped forward and said he would pay the tickets and fines due. He handed the Trenitalia employee his credit card which he quickly snatched out of Brett's hand. Ilene and I insisted Brett not pay anything, but he just smiled, winked, and told us not to worry about a thing. He would explain why later—away from the employee. After returning Brett's credit card, the employee put on a wry smile and started to walk away.

During this entire event, Ally was upset, as we all were. She was also filming the whole episode on her phone. Suddenly, the employee quickly turned toward Ally and tried to grab her phone from her. I stepped between them and would not let him approach her, plus if you knew our daughter, she had no intention of giving it to him anyway. As we walked away, he kept insisting—emphatically—that the incident be removed from Ally's phone. I looked him straight in the eyes and told him that wasn't going to happen. He wasn't a happy camper.

As soon as we walked down the steps to leave the station, Ilene and I are eager to learn Brett's logic and his lack of concern over the episode. Brett informed us the charge had already been canceled from his account and the belligerent employee will never know. When using a foreign bank card there's a window of about thirty minutes before the card gets "technically" charged. When the charge appeared to go through on the employee's tablet screen, Brett waited a few seconds and canceled it. The best part? The rude, unpleasant Trenitalia employee never even knew what happened.

I know this sounds like we're beating Trenitalia out of four fares, but we offered to pay what we owed before the fiasco started. It was the insistence of the employee, along with his brassy attitude which led to Brett's action. Truly an innocent mistake on our part as we are veteran train travelers, this was a rooky blunder we often tell others not to make. Ilene just didn't want us to miss our lunch reservations or hurry through exploring the other town. Making our way down the path to the harbor, we were still shaking our heads and talking about the incident.

While touring the main street of Vernazza, we passed by a store selling pizza and, of course, we stopped for a slice. Yes, our lunch reservations were in thirty minutes but as Brett said, it smelled so good he needed a slice. Since I couldn't let him eat alone, I devoured one too. As I said, the man loves pizza.

We toured the harbor area, and sat on the rocks for a few minutes, before heading for our reservation at Ristorante Belforte. Giovanni told me to ask for a table with Andrea, pronunciation [an-DRAY-uh] as our waiter and we did. If you ever visited Vernazza you'd recognize this restaurant. It sits high on the cliffs overlooking the harbor and is noted for its seafood and breathtaking views.

As we introduced ourselves to the owner at the desk, she asked us to wait for a moment so they could set a table for us. We met our waiter Andrea, and all I can say is, let the show begin—and it did. I've experienced the good fortune and opportunity to meet many waiters in my years, but I never met someone who loves his job as Andrea does. He led us through a narrow doorway. The small, natural cut out patio held only a few tables perched directly over the sea. We were so close to the water, we heard the waves crashing against the rocks underneath, and occasionally, felt a drop or two from the pounding water.

The color of the sea dazzled in varied, multiple shades of blue and turquoise with ships and sailboats visible off in the distance. *Things don't get much better than this,* I thought to myself. Glancing in Ilene's direction, Andrea inquired if we were happy with the setting. He could tell by the ear-to-ear smile that she was very pleased. Ally asked if she could sit closer to the building instead of over the water as she's somewhat fearful of heights. With a little rearranging, Ilene and I sat at the railing side of the table.

Before I tell you about the food, let me tell you about Andrea. I said earlier he's a man who loves his job but, that alone would be an understatement. As a waiter, he's excellent. His knowledge of the menu is second to none. His recommendations were also spot on, but the best part became the show he puts on for his guests. Every time he leaves your table, whether for food, wine, or to deliver a utensil, he reappears, wearing a different hat. For clarification, I don't mean just a regular hat, such as a fedora or a panama hat, I mean funny hats and he has plenty of them. One's a pirate hat, another a crab hat with buggy eyes on it, and yet another with a flamingo with a long neck. Andrea has quite a collection of funny hats that his customers have sent him over the years. He also likes to sing, so don't be surprised if you're serenaded with a few lines from a song or two. He's very attentive to his customers' needs and creates a great atmosphere to enjoy a great meal.

Now, about the food. Belforte specializes in seafood, and it makes perfect sense given its location on the Mediterranean Sea. We each ordered a different entrée assuming there would be some sharing. Ally and Brett ordered a tuna appetizer, a bowl of muscles cooked in a white wine sauce and stacked high on the plate, pasta with pesto, and a shrimp dish, although I can't recall the details. Ilene and I ordered a Caprese salad with artichokes as a starter. Ilene's choice—spaghetti alle vongole, clams in a white wine sauce with more clams than I've ever seen on this dish before, and I happily ordered the *polpo,* octopus. I love octopus and try to order it whenever I see it on the menu, especially at a good seafood restaurant. I fell in love with the very first bite and it only progressed from there. Of course, we each shared tastes, and I can honestly say that the food was exceptional. Ally and Brett travel all over the world, so for them to say their food was one of the best they've enjoyed, was a glowing report. Of course, Ilene and I thought so too. We'll go back to Belforte again, not only for the food but to visit Andrea, the waiter too.

Bellies full, we decided to head back to the train station and continue with our trip. Next stop, Riomaggiore, the stop we missed which started the whole train fiasco. Since Ally and Brett had never traveled to the Cinque Terre area, Ilene and I wanted to show them one more town before heading back to Lucca. Thankfully, the next leg of our trip was uneventful, without any additional drama—no arguments on the platform.

We climbed down steps and traveled through a pretty tunnel to the sea area. Ilene and I didn't remember walking through a tunnel before.

"This must be new," Ilene said, "it's been several years since we've visited here."

Spending some time down by the water relaxing, quietly watching the sea meet the rocks and some men fishing, this area is completely different from the view in Vernazza's harbor. It's extremely rocky and narrow. Each of these five little towns boasts a different character and it would have been wonderful to introduce these two to each one of them.

Back in the main part of the town, we enjoyed exploring some shops. Ally and Brett wanted to buy some souvenirs for friends and family back home. While walking the empty streets, it dawned on me, that we'd reached the time of day, *siesta,* when things shut down—even tourist towns. Heading back to Lucca we decided we'd had enough excitement for one day. Ideally, it would've been terrific to show them more of these five little towns, but we just didn't allocate enough time. If they'd stayed in Lucca longer, we would've spent the night in one of the towns to explore more of the area. Our motto? Always leave something for a return visit.

❧ Panzano ❧

I checked into renting a car for the day, but prices were extremely high. By the time you add tolls and gas, it wasn't much more to hire a private driver to take us to Panzano. This would also enable me to enjoy some Chianti wine without any concerns. Panzano is a two-and-a-half-hour drive from Lucca through the beautiful Chianti countryside. I love driving through this part of Italy and seeing vineyards off in the distance with the rows of vines perfectly aligned. Long, winding dirt roads lined with Etruscan pines leading to a palazzo, or villa, where someone lives. The endless shimmer of grey and green olive groves also in rows flowed over the hills. I've often dreamt of living in a vineyard such as these, but I'm content to enjoy the fruits of their labors and savor their wines. As they say… It's a tough job, but someone has to do it.

Arriving into town and after our driver took a wrong turn, he stopped on a small, narrow street to ask for directions. Noticing two women speaking to men sitting on the steps of an apartment building, he lowered down the passenger window. Leaning over and before he could say a word, one of the women asked him if he was looking for Dario Cecchini's shop. She pointed, giving him directions where we needed to turn. I guess this little town gets plenty of visitors looking for Dario's. Navigating with the proper directions, we arrived at our destination a few moments later.

We exited the car, right outside Dario's butcher shop, and the first person to greet us? A lovely young lady carrying about fifteen stacked jelly-jar style glasses in one hand and a gallon jug of wine in the other. She asked if we would like some wine. Obviously, she didn't know me. We each took a glass from her arms, as she poured. At that moment, I started thinking about how much I love this town. There's a very nice piazza just down the street from Dario's and since Panzano is a hilltop town there are some beautiful views of the valley and towns below. It's probably one of the smallest towns in the Chianti region, but it has one thing the others lack—Dario Cecchini. Thousands of visitors come to this area each year. Dario's mission is to spread his love of meat, but also to share his deep respect for animals. His establishments are divided into several parts. The butcher shop, and three restaurants which together, use every part of an animal.

As soon as our wine was poured, Ally and Brett headed in the direction of the souvenir shop. Ilene and I peeked into the butcher shop window trying to catch a glimpse of the man himself—Dario. As luck would have it, he was sitting on a small stool in the corner behind the meat case display. Ilene and I set out for the souvenir shop to catch up with Ally and Brett, figuring we'd all walk in together. Brett has a friend back in the States who's a huge Dario fan, and a chef himself. When Ally and Brett told him we were going to eat at his restaurant, he was pretty jealous. Souvenirs were bought for their chef friend and themselves, and we headed to the butcher shop together. Diners actually enter the restaurant through the butcher shop.

As we entered, Ilene caught Dario's eye and said in a not-so-shy voice, "*Mio marito*, my husband's a *macellaio*, butcher, too."

At once he rose from his seat and scurried to the front of the meat case. As he approached us, I realized he was quite a bit taller and broader than I expected. Hand extended and with a huge smile on his face he greeted us and grabbed my hand like we were long-lost friends. We did the Italian hug thing and started a conversation.

He asked where in the States I trained as a butcher as his relatives live in Brooklyn. I told him I worked for a family-run shop in Elmhurst, Queens from the age of fourteen till twenty-six years old. Ilene asked if he would mind taking a group picture with all of us. In Italian, he asked the lovely young lady who served us wine to take it for us.

With Ally on one side of me and Dario on the other, something funny was said between the three of us, and we all started laughing. Several photos were taken—all with us in hysterics—all except Brett and Ilene, who stood at the other end of the photo line. They were clueless about the reason for the uproar. I don't even recall what created such laughter… it's photos like this that create memories. We were both so happy that Dario agreed to use this photo in this book—and include his recipe!

Ilene always says, "… Because every photo tells a story." It's true.

Dario requested if just he and I could take a picture and of course, I obliged. There I stood, grinning from ear to ear taking a photo with my new friend and loving every moment of it. As we all stood there just talking with Dario, we were informed that the restaurant was now open, and that we should follow the hostess to our seats. I once again shook Dario's hand and told him how very pleased I was to meet him.

As we walked through the shop, we were led through the meat-cutting area with butcher blocks, meat grinders, and an array of knives and cleavers. I'm comfortable walking through the cutting area as it reminded me of the shop where I worked, Lester's Market in Elmhurst. I could almost see Harry and Billy standing there ready to start our day. A sense of nostalgia overcame me, and I must have had a wistful smile on my face because Ilene asked if all was all right.

I just looked at her, putting her mind to ease, and answered, "Of course, I'm in a butcher shop."

Up the steps, we went following our hostess to our table. It's a long communal table—family style, and we were seated near the grill. The room's long and narrow and quickly became packed with other visitors all looking to savor the upcoming meal. Each table's group setting included some veggies in a bucket, bread, and of course a gallon jug of Chianti wine. Immediately after we sat down the first course began.

The beef carpaccio's prepared perfectly and delicious. We chose the beef option for lunch because Brett doesn't eat pork and to tell the truth, I would've chosen this menu anyway. After the carpaccio, the grilled meats ensued, one by one. We enjoyed a total of five different cuts of beef, each prepared perfectly, and each cut tasted delicious. I remember being told by a few acquaintances the meal wasn't great, and you're just hoping to meet Dario. Well, let me say here and now, that nothing could be further from the truth. The beef was so juicy and mouthwatering, and the baked potato… divine—that's right, I said divine. The orange pound cake for dessert happened to be delicious too. Oh, and did I mention the gallon of Chianti at each table? It wasn't a Chianti Classico, but a very good *rosso* table wine and we all showed signs of enjoying all of it, the food—the wine, and the service.

After the meal, Dario came upstairs to greet everyone. He stopped right behind where I'm seated, put his chin on top of my head, gave me a big hug, and ask if everything met my standards. *My standards* are as though I'm a renowned food critic or someone of importance.

I answered, "Yes, of course, it did, and I did not expect anything less. Since we now live in Lucca, we will return more often."

Then instantly the unexpected happened. He kissed me on the top of my head and said, "*Grazie Mille,* thank you very much and he looked forward to seeing us again."

Okay, the kiss on the head came across as a little strange but heartfelt, and I believe my praise of his establishment meant something to him. The only problem—Ilene missed the whole episode as she stepped away to visit the powder room. Luckily, Ally captured the whole encounter on her cellphone, so at least Ilene was able to enjoy the event by watching the video.

If you are in Tuscany, I highly recommend a visit to Dario's restaurant, Antica Macelleria Cecchini. Please be forewarned… make sure you bring your appetite, you will need it and more importantly, bring your best smile. Dario and his staff will appreciate it.

Thanks to our friend Lita, she provided Ilene with Dario's recipe for the orange cake. She's made it with Vin Santo and Amara and we've loved both of them. By the way, Brett loved Ilene's version of the cake too.

Dario's Orange Olive Oil Pound Cake

Ingredients:
3 large eggs
1¼ cup + ¼ cup sugar, keep measurements separate
1 small orange
5 ounces olive oil
⅓ cup Vin Santo, Brandy, or Amara liquor
⅓ cup water
2¼ cups all-purpose flour
3½ teaspoons baking powder
¼ cup of raisins (I've been known to use a more)

Directions:
1. Preheat oven to 355°
2. Using an electric mixer, beat 1¼ cups of the sugar along with eggs very well.
3. Chop the orange (whole, including peel and pulp) into small pieces and mix it with the oil, add the Vin Santo (or other liquor), and water. Add these liquid ingredients to the egg and sugar mixture.
4. Combine the flour and baking powder; then incorporate them into the batter, a little at a time, until well-blended.
5. Prepare the pan (loaf pan) by liberally buttering and flouring the surface.
6. Pour the mixture into the pan and add the raisins.
7. Level the batter, covering the raisins so they don't burn.
8. Sprinkle with the remaining ¼ cup of sugar on top of the batter.
9. Bake for 40 minutes, or until done with a toothpick test. Don't let it burn.

☙

We planned a leisurely day since Ally and Brett were leaving the following morning. Knowing they still needed to pack, we wanted a relaxing, peaceful chunk of time for them to chill. Sitting at the table Ilene asked Ally if she would like to see or do something last minute.

Ally replied, "Let's go shopping on Via Fillungo."

I'm a bit surprised at Ally's answer as I was about to suggest something else to do but Ilene chimed in with, "Sounds like a great idea."

I glanced over at Brett for his reaction and response. His expression indicated he was fine with it. Now, I don't mind walking down Via Fillungo, but shopping with the three of them might torture me. Oh well, as the saying goes, when in Rome.

Brett likes to spoil Ally and he will buy her pretty much whatever she wants. As a parent, I should be happy he's this way as my daughter's the beneficiary of his generosity but seriously, how many pairs of shoes or sunglasses does a person need? Well, I guess she wanted more shoes because when we returned to the apartment I counted a total of six boxes—five for Ally and one for Ilene and a few other items thrown in for the heck of it. I became the proud owner of a new blue belt thanks to Ally's spending spree and the need to use up a EUR 40,00 bonus credit in one store… and a pair of very tired feet. To this day when Ilene and I walk past the shops where the carnage took place, we are greeted with waving arms and big smiles.

☙

When we arrived home from shopping Brett checked his email. The airlines informed them their flight had been canceled until the following day. This meant another day with the two of them, which pleased Ilene and me. The news brought big smiles to our faces. Luckily for Ilene, it also meant Brett could help her with the new computer she bought a month ago. She bought a Mac, completely different from the Windows PC we are both used to. Since both Ally and Brett are "Mac people," helping Ilene became the quest of the day.

ᴓ

One problem though, their flight the following day meant they would need to secure COVID tests on a Sunday instead of Saturday. Almost all *farmacie* are closed for testing on Sunday, even the hospitals. We secured a time on Sunday for them at the Pisa airport which does COVID testing seven days a week. With the problem solved we're able to continue enjoying the kids and working on Ilene's computer.

ᴓ

Ilene wasn't feeling one hundred percent on Sunday, so I took Ally and Brett on the train to the Pisa airport. This will supply a good test run for us as we've never traveled to the airport in Pisa this way. A simple transfer from the Pisa Centrale railway station to the high-speed, fully automatic People Mover service took us directly to the airport. It was quick and easy. Tests were done and negative, it was an easy trip back to Lucca to enjoy the rest of the day.

ᴓ

Monday morning's somewhat of a sad day for Ilene and me. It meant we needed to say goodbye to the kids and it's always a hard thing to do. We'd reveled in the fun, and loved every moment spent with them, so parting's always bittersweet. Just like when they visited us in Florence, the car picked them up at the apartment, we all said our goodbyes, and off they went. As usual, tears came to our eyes as we walked up the steps to our now very quiet apartment. It's back to just the two of us and it's all right, we understand all good things must come to an end.

On the brighter side, we'll see them in London this coming October for five days. Brett has a speaking engagement there and asked if we would like to join them in London. We didn't hesitate, and we look forward to enjoying our own private tour guide, Brett. He lived in London for five years and we'll happily be the beneficiaries of his knowledge of the city. You know, October's not too far off which made saying goodbye this time a lot easier. I'm looking forward to drinking room-temperature beer with my fish and chips and being with the kids again. *A presto*, see you soon, Ally and Brett.

ଓ

Ilene

A surprise email brings a smile to my face and when I opened it, I hollered to Gary, "Where are you? I've something to tell you."

I know our apartment's only three rooms, but I didn't want to utter the entire conversation out loud. When Gary appeared in the bedroom doorway, I told him I received an email from Joanie. Joanie was a former co-worker when I was a principal's secretary for the Paradise Valley Unified School District in Phoenix, Arizona. We both worked at Sunrise and later, Mountain Trail Middle School. Joanie was one of those special teachers I looked forward to seeing every day. She always knew how to put a smile on my face—she was just a great start to my day. I would hand her the list of any absent teachers for the day, and she would write them on the whiteboard in the teachers' lounge—a way of informing staff members who wasn't on campus that day.

"She and John were on a cruise and coming to Lucca," I excitedly told Gary.

At the beginning of this story, you might recall that we were going to take a cruise home with a couple after our seven months in Italy. Of course, with the pandemic, they didn't take the cruise, and we wound up staying in Italy. These same friends were now finally coming to "the boot." They'd dock in Livorno and take a day tour to Pisa and Lucca.

With only a few hours to spend in Lucca, we needed to make each moment count. Although it was a school day for us and the last week of school, I couldn't imagine them coming to Lucca and not seeing them. It just wasn't going to happen. I texted our teacher and told her both Gary and I wouldn't be attending school. We were only allowed to text in Italian, so my message, *"Gary e io non scuola oggie,"* wasn't one hundred percent correct but I hoped it was enough to convey the message.

The day arrived and we found out Joanie's husband, John, wasn't feeling well and would be staying on board the ship. Disappointed, we texted Joanie to find out where the tour bus would let the group off outside the wall in Lucca. After a few back-and-forth messages, we confirmed it's Porta San Pietro on the south side of Lucca Centro. Arriving, we walked through the porta looking for her and her tour group. Gary spotted the bus and a few people walking around it, but how could we be certain it was them—the correct group? Gary decided to go back inside the wall after we didn't spot Joanie right away. I heard Gary whistle and I assume he'd found her. As I walked back inside the porta, I spotted Gary hugging her, and picked up my pace. I threw my arms around her and gave her a long hug, beaming with happiness to see my dear friend again.

She introduced us to friends on the tour and the tour leader who happened to be from Lucca. Joanie decided to ditch the group tour and come on a private tour with us, including our apartment. We confirmed the time we needed to return to this same location and set off down the street.

As we walked through the streets, we pointed out some of the major attractions and piazzas in Lucca. Stopping at our favorite store, Taddeucci, I stepped inside to buy a loaf of buccellato bread for her to enjoy with friends on the bus, and with John as well. Buccellato is a traditional sweet bread of Lucca. It's made with sugar, raisins, and aniseed. Created back in Roman times as bread for the soldiers, it's said, "Whoever comes to Lucca and does not eat buccellato, is like never having been there." We always buy a loaf for special people as we walk the streets on a guided, private tour.

Stepping out on Via Fillungo, we headed toward Piazza Anfiteatro and showed her inside. The piazza was bustling with people shopping and eating in restaurants. As we walked through and back on the main street, we took her to see one of the passageways underneath the wall. To us, it's beautiful. Probably not something exceptional, but we love the history of why these openings or passageways are there. Joanie's quite impressed and loves the structure.

"I don't think this was on your friend's tour," I said to her.

Arriving at our apartment, she understood why we've chosen this place as our home. It's small but charming and when she saw the terrace, she smiled as we did when we first saw it too. We sat and relaxed a bit. It's great to hear about people back in Arizona whom we both know. Sitting there on this beautiful day, I thought to myself, *has time stood still?* It seemed like no time has passed since our last face-to-face conversation. Of course, it had—it just didn't seem like it though. What is it about the perception of time at this stage of our lives? It either moves extremely quickly or just the opposite. This experience of time is so strange.

We didn't want Joanie to arrive late and hold up her group, so we completed the tour in plenty of time to stop and enjoy a drink at a bar on the street near the porta, where she needed to meet the others in her group. Spending the day catching up with Joanie was wonderful, although we were sad John couldn't make the trip too. As the others approached the bus where we waited, tears welled up in my eyes. It was time for her to leave and return to the ship in Livorno. We thanked her for choosing Lucca to visit over another tour she could've chosen. We'd see them again when we returned to Arizona.

☙

There are a few things I'd like to make for the apartment and decided it might be time to investigate sewing machines in Italy. I do own a nice one back in Arizona, but it would be too heavy to ship. Besides, and you've probably already experienced this before if you've traveled here, the different electric system in Italy is problematic. Items with motors bought elsewhere, don't afford longevity here.

Since traveling to Italy, we've bought a blow dryer, hair clippers, and an immersion blender due to the fact the ones we brought years ago blew up. Literally. The voltage in Europe is more powerful, and it takes a toll on appliances. Converters work, but not usually with motorized items, and not for any great length of time.

Our apartment has two different plugs too. It's an issue with older homes throughout Italy. We've several small and fat three-prong outlets in all the rooms. You can usually use a two-prong in the three-prong outlet, but it requires the same size pin. Besides, that is too much current flowing through the appliance. Generally, we always use a power strip where most of our electronics are stationed—usually the desk. This way, we use the correct converter to plug in our power strip and all our American plugs fit into the strip itself. I've veered off the main subject—sewing.

Gary and I prefer to patronize local shops rather than big box stores as we call them in the States. It's difficult, but I try not to use online shopping as a first resort. It's just how we roll. I understand the convenience of online shopping, but especially after seeing businesses in Italy struggle to stay open after the pandemic, we try—we don't always succeed—but we try.

After finding a quilting store outside the wall in the San Concordio area, Gary and I rode our bicycles to investigate. The store is adorable, filled with bolts of beautiful fabrics, sewing notions, and machines. I'm taken aback, just a little, and stood in the doorway to take it all in. It wasn't a JoAnn Fabrics retail store like back in the States, but they offer quite a selection of nice quality, cotton fabrics. I took in a deep breath. Wandering around the store, the owner approached us and said something to us in Italian.

I understood most of what she was asking, but I did say, *"Lei parla Inglese?"* do you speak English?

The owner raised her hand and using her thumb and index finger slightly apart from one another, she indicated she speaks a little. Perfect, a little English goes a long way.

I inquired about sewing machines and she carried some nice Juki and Brothers but more of a machine than I needed to buy. I didn't need thirty fancy stitches anymore; those days are gone. As I looked around the small shop, I spotted a large, free-standing quilting rail system and long-arm sewing machine. I glanced over at Gary and smirked. My favorite part of quilting is deciding on a pattern, choosing the material, and watching it turn into a piece of art. The quilting part itself doesn't do it for me. This could be the answer to my dreams. The owner told me she could quilt my project for me or teach me how to do it. I'm thrilled. After finding out the prices of her basic machines—I wasn't so thrilled. As much as I wanted to help her out and patronize her shop, I'm forced to buy a machine on the Internet, but I could buy thread, fabric, and supplies from her. Returning home, I bought my trusty Singer online.

ღ

We've met so many wonderful people in Italy during several of our trips. Believe it or not, most of them we keep in contact with through email, texts, or us sending greeting cards. Not American's but true Italians. Each has touched our hearts differently, but each has left a mark of some kind and created memories we will never forget.

One such special person is Francesca. Our "adopted" Italian daughter who used to work and live in Florence, where we first met her years ago. She made the ninety days we spent in Florence special—she is special and has been from the moment we met her. She managed a restaurant while acquiring her degree in counseling. She loves speaking English with us as it helps her with her studies. Since then, she's moved back to her hometown of Prato where her family's from and still lives.

We were delighted to learn that Francesca is now living closer to Lucca, just up in the hills in a small town, and would love to see us again. Our planned trip a few months ago was canceled as her parents weren't feeling well. I knew we would eventually reunite but it couldn't happen soon enough for me. I love her smile, her abundance of energy, and her kindness.

One day, I received a text from her, telling us that one of her friends would be singing in a restaurant just outside the north wall of Lucca Centro, and would we like to meet her there? *Of course, we would!* I've held a signed copy of our first book with a private inscription we never mailed to her due to the cost from the States. Thinking of our friend Joel, we asked him if he'd like to join us for an evening out with a glass of vino while listening to Francesca's friend perform. He agreed. Fortunately, it was a quick ten-minute walk to the restaurant's location.

Spotting Francesca walking down the street brought a huge smile to my face. Her hair was longer now, while still looking as lovely as ever. With long hugs and kisses, I finally let her go to get a good look at her by holding our arms stretched out wide. I tilted my head and smiled... it's so good to see her again. After the second round of *baci,* kisses between Gary and me, we introduced her to Joel. Just as we concluded introductions, Francesca's friend appeared at the door and another round of formalities was in order.

Stepping inside, we found out Francesca's friend reserved the front table for all of us. We waited until the song ended before slipping into our seats. She's a guest singer with a saxophone and keyboard player. Francesca ordered a scrumptious charcuterie board and wine for the table.

At midnight, it was time to call it a night. This delightful evening had been ideal, filled with good food, wine, music, and reuniting with a woman we lovingly refer to as our adopted Italian daughter. As we stepped outside the door, I stopped, took both my open palms and placed them on both her cheeks.

"Let's not wait so long to see you again." "*Ti voglio bene, Francesca—ti voglio bene.*" This phrase means: I love you to a friend in Italian. I meant it with all my heart.

∽ Shopping with Pasquale ∾
Gary

One Sunday evening as Ilene and I began relaxing to watch some television, I received a text message from our good friend Giacomo. He asked If I wanted to join him and Pasquale on Tuesday to shop at the Mercato.

I remember looking at Ilene and saying something like, "I made it, I made the club."

Giacomo and Pasquale hold a special friendship and they do things together like going to the Mercato or wine tastings. No one else, just the two of them. The invitation to join them was unexpected since I didn't know Pasquale well, but I wasn't about to turn it down.

This particular Mercato is the equivalent of Costco in the States and Pasquale does most of his food and supply shopping for the restaurant there. The invitation was a big deal, and an honor for me. We would meet and leave from Pasquale's restaurant at nine o'clock.

As Giacomo and I arrived, we were told we'd leave closer to ten because first Pasquale needed to go pick up his fish order. He made us espresso and left for a few moments. When Pasquale arrived back at the restaurant, we helped him unload the fish and sat and enjoyed another espresso. Now I love espresso and enjoy one every morning, but I'm now up to my third cup in the last hour and strange things started happening to my body. I haven't experienced this much energy in a long time.

As we arrived at the Mercato, I figured I would just follow Pasquale's lead since he knows his way around. Giacomo and I grabbed a cart which costs one euro. This euro is returned to you after you return the cart. The cart attendant brought Pasquale a cart and greeted him with a personal "Buongiorno." *Impressive* I thought to myself. He has some pull here. As we entered the store, I'm surprised, as it did look like a Costco. They've also quite a few things you will not find in the States. There's a section of just cheeses, I mean entire, whole wheels of Reggiano Parmigiana, and about any other cheese you could want. There's a meat section with a choice of beef, pork, and veal from countries all over the world. The wine area has one of the largest selections I've encountered in Italy. It's an amazing place to shop and the selections are endless.

Our first stop was the fresh fish section since his fish guy earlier in the day didn't produce everything Pasquale wanted for the menu that evening. Next up was the cheese section and what an education this became. As Pasquale walked through each section, he would recommend a product or two and explain why. Once he found what he needed, he'd take off to the next zone.

A few times when Giacomo and I conversed about a product and returned to the cart, we noticed Pasquale had disappeared. It would be difficult to lose someone in this store, but the guy resembles a fantom shopper, here one minute and gone the next. Giacomo told me he's like this all the time so he just tries to keep up as best he can.

Approaching the meat area and looking at the choices of filets on the table, we weren't pleased with the overall selection, and Pasquale wasn't either. So, before we knew it, Pasquale walked into the cutting room, then reappeared with six different wrapped filets, laid them on the display table, and asked me if these looked better. The guy has purchased filets for years and he was now asking me for my opinion since I once was a butcher. I told him which filets I thought appeared the best and why. He added two to his cart, while Giacomo and I took one to split. Both our freezers are not large enough to hold an entire filet of steak. We will often split the cost of a filet which allows each of us a few meals without trying to be creative and find extra freezer space.

The pace began to slow down a bit as we arrived at the wine section. Giacomo is a certified Italian wine expert and Pasquale is a sommelier. Going through the wine section with the two of them became one heck of an education. Not only did I acquire knowledge on wine, but Pasquale will tell you if the price is high, fair, or low, and if the production year is a good year for the wine. At this point, my head felt like it was going to explode from the information overload.

We stopped at a few more sections and finally, the time arrived to check out. Packing the car, Pasquale said he needed to make a few more stops. Next up—is Carrefour, a French grocery chain.

☙

As we entered the store, Pasquale offered to buy us espresso, so we agree. I mean you need the energy just to keep up with him. He says this stop will be fast as he only needs to buy some fresh ricotta. He only buys his ricotta cheese here—period. As we walked toward the cheese case, Pasquale is interrupted by six or seven people saying hello to him. I looked at Giacomo and inquired if this scenario was normal. He nodded in the affirmative, the guy knows people everywhere you go. At the cheese case, he did not see what he wanted so he walked into the refrigerated room at the back of the store and came out holding six kilos of fresh ricotta cheese.

☙

Our next stop—Esselunga, another big supermarket chain store, and another "quick stop," according to Pasquale… since he only needs to buy some bread. When we walked into the store, Pasquale is greeted by at least five more people—none of whom worked in the store. When we walked up to the bakery section, he put twenty loaves of bread, five without sesame seeds, and fifteen with seeds into his cart. At this point, even though I'd had five espresso, I'm exhausted and could not wait to return home to relax.

☙

I've cherished the pleasure of accompanying Pasquale several times and enjoy every time I go with him and Giacomo. It's a bonding experience for the three of us, which I understand Pasquale enjoys too. I wish I were younger so I could keep up with him. The man is the Energizer Bunny—non-stop motion and a lot of fun to shop with.

Chiavari
Ilene

When in Lucca in November 2019, we wanted to visit the town of Chiavari. Our friend, fellow blogger, and ex-pat Marilyn lives there, and we just love her photos. When Gary and I visited, she had been back in the States—but we enjoyed exploring her little town anyway.

With the weather so beautiful, and before the heat truly set in, we arranged to finally meet. The three-hour train ride from Lucca to Chiavari was long—but beautiful. I worked a little on my Italian while watching the beauty of small towns pass by my window. Seeing the Carrara Mountains reminds me of an upcoming trip we'd like to book. I sighed. My bucket list is so long and little by little we are chipping away at it. I'm delighted.

Exiting the train, we spot Marilyn right away with a big smile on her pretty face. Sticky from the train ride, we lightly hug. We swiftly began chatting like we were old friends who've known each other for years. Such a comfortable feeling when you "know someone" whom you've never met in person. We experience this a great deal. It's heartwarming.

As we walked the streets of Chiavari, I'm reminded of how much I enjoyed visiting this town. The architecture is fabulous and the *trompe l'oeil* style of paintings are abundant. It's a French style of painting that represents an object which deceives the eye. There are "fake" windows, molding, and decorative elements adorning buildings. The colors are vivid without being bright as you find in Burano, Venice. I sighed again.

The central market was in full swing with vendors selling produce, flowers, and jars of honey, jams, and jellies. I also spotted a stand with pots of various herbs for sale. I paused to take it all in, but I wasn't ready to buy anything that day.

The last time we visited, the *duomo* was closed, so I'm excited to see the doors open. Open doors are always an opportunity. We stepped inside. I paused at the doorway—taken aback by the complexity of the interior. Styled in Baroque architecture, I'm overwhelmed. After taking a photo from the back of the church, I walked up the center aisle. Nooks and crannies were filled with cherubs and figures all in gold. The ceiling is stunning with amazing, detailed frescoes. There wasn't a section not decorated to some extent. My eyes tried to take it all in, but my emotions got the better of me. I sat in a pew to say a brief prayer. After raising my head, I caught of glimpse of Marilyn and Gary on one side of the church and joined them.

"It's a lot to take in," said Marilyn as if she read my mind, and I agreed. After dozens of pictures, we headed back outside, squinting as we exited.

A bit hungry from the long train ride, Marilyn suggested a local place to enjoy lunch. As we entered the outdoor seating area, the menu is being written in chalk on a board hanging outside the entrance to the restaurant. *Just the way I like it.* This means everything's fresh and probably bought today in the market. As the woman writes in the prices, I smiled. Affordable *and* fresh—today we were in for a treat.

What could be better than to enjoy some fantastic local food and find out more about our friend? Lunch functions as an event in Italy. You can sit and relax at your table for thirty minutes or hours. It doesn't matter. Well, it matters if they are going to close between lunch and dinner, but this wasn't the case.

Heading toward the waterfront, I spot several buildings I took pictures of during our previous visit. The memory brought a smile to my face. Arriving on the wide, flat, stone promenade, we view several brave souls in the water. It's a hot day, about ninety degrees Fahrenheit, but I always assume the water is still chilly. The Gulf of Tigullio can't be more than about seventy-two degrees.

Chiavari's only about twenty minutes south of Genova. As I start taking a few photos, Marilyn points out Portofino just around the bay at the tip of the gulf. I squint and spot a very large yacht in the distance and confirm with Marilyn it's exactly Portofino's location. She mentioned that the bay encountered major congestion with the number of yachts present when Kourtney Kardashian married Travis Barker in Portofino several weeks ago. Several helicopters also filled the skies and scanned the area. Hollywood's just not my scene, so I casually waved my hand in dismissal. Easily spotted as well, is the sea town of Santa Margherita, just to the right of Portofino.

We stepped into the gelato store, and each ordered our favorites. Finding a bench along the promenade, we enjoyed the beautiful scenery and conversation. The sun was shining, and while soaking up all its warmth, it was a wonderful day to be outside. I resisted the temptation to put my feet in the water, but it was lovely to be near it again. The view of the sea captivated me in unimaginable ways. I'm in awe of nature's beauty—its sense of peace and serenity. We wrap up our day, and invite Marilyn to visit Lucca one day in the future and to keep in touch.

On the train home, I thought to myself, *I might enjoy living in Chiavari.* Although there isn't much English spoken in the town, I would love to be by the water and enjoy a small motorboat to go fishing. Interesting as I've not thought about any other town other than Lucca since we arrived.

Modena

We welcomed another road trip with Gianna and Giacomo on a beautiful day the first of June. Today's adventure? To the Emilia-Romagna region—known for its balsamic vinegar, opera heritage, and Ferrari and Lamborghini Italian sports cars.

The first stop is the Ferrari Maranello Museum. Gary and I both enjoyed the Enzo Museum which focuses on the life and work of Enzo Ferrari. Gianna thought this museum would supply a different perspective for us as the museum in Maranello focuses more on the history and evolution of the Ferrari car design. We're excited.

Even though I'm not a big "sports car person," I do appreciate nice design. Ferraris are a thing of beauty—that's for sure. We entered the museum, and the sea of red is broken by just a few other colors. One in sunny yellow, a silver, and an unusual one in a softer blue color with a white stripe down the center. Detailed information is provided with each car displayed, along with countless photos and memorabilia mounted along the perimeter walls. For a reasonable cost, there are even opportunities to take your photo in a Ferrari, as well as have fun driving in several simulators. After taking our time on the self-tour through the museum and taking dozens of photos and videos, we grabbed a quick lunch while we waited for the bus tour to begin.

This shuttle bus tour took us from the museum to the Ferrari factory just down the street. You are not allowed inside the factory, and in fact, you don't even exit the bus. No photos or videos are allowed during the tour. The guide spoke in both Italian and English, describing what we were seeing driving down the main street, "Viale Enzo Ferrari." She explained each building's purpose as the bus paused in front. We could see workers, some in red uniforms, walking from building to building. Everyone sported a noticeable badge. They keep this place under tight security.

Exiting the factory area, we drove through town to another area and enter another security checkpoint. Gary and I looked at each other and we realized this had every indication of being the famous Fiorano Circuit. This would interest me. This private racetrack is owned by Ferrari for the development and training of drivers and mechanics, and where vehicles are tested and calibrated. The length of this circuit equals 3,021 meters or 1.88 miles, and the average speed is more than 99 miles per hour—with peaks of more than 180 miles per hour. The guide informed us that many curves on this track are replications of other famous track embankments from actual races held around the world.

The bus traveled around the track and paused while all eyes are glued to the windows. In a flash, I saw something out of the corner of my eye pass so quickly, that it was just a blur. *What was that?* I wondered. I heard "*oohs* and *ahhs*" from the other tour passengers.

I whispered to Gary, "What did I miss?"

He leaned over to me and muttered, "Keep watching, it's coming around again."

In an instant, I saw it. It was a car, but the water on the track created the soaring spray of water that first caught my attention. The guide informed us they were testing the tires, but she said it in such a way that made me wonder, *are they just testing the tires for rain?*

We watched the one car travel the circuit for several minutes before moving on and back to the museum parking lot. The tour had been enjoyable and the day with these two friends, couldn't have been better. *Or could it?*

ꕥ

Balsamic Vinegar

From the Ferrari Museum, they took us to a place they've visited, and enjoyed, many times before. They wanted us to experience it too. It's a short drive through the beautiful countryside before arriving at the beautiful front gates of Antica Acetaia Cavedoni—just in time for our reservation.

Marcello greeted all of us with a big, warm smile. While waiting for the other small group to arrive, he shows us the nearby vines on the property. The land is glorious and spreads up far onto the hills around this beautiful stone building. Entering the building, there's a long, rustic table set for our two groups. As I look around, I'm trying to take it all in… I can feel the history of this family in this room, which dates to 1860. The large black and white photographs of past generations line the far wall. Marcello introduced us to his family—going all the way back several generations. As though it's choreographed and planned, at almost the perfect moment, he introduced us to his father, Paolo, who appeared at the doorway. Handshakes all around, this looked like a wonderful family business—yet it wasn't always so. Marcello tells us the family always produced the balsamic for themselves and as gifts. It wasn't until just a few years ago, that he convinced his father they could make it a business.

The other group arrived—a young family with two children about seven and ten along with a grandparent. We introduce ourselves. They are Americans. Of course, I can't recall where they were from, but it doesn't matter in the big scheme of things.

The tour began with Marcello taking us to another room. Small wooden barrels, unlike very large wine barrels, are lined up in rows. They are extremely dark in color, an indicator of their age per Marcello. At this point, I saw it for myself. Gianna previously related the story to me about this family and how special they are. Since they had visited this family business several times before, they lingered at the back of the group. My position was at the front of the group, I leaned slightly back to catch Gianna's eye. She smiled back. At this point, I saw it for myself. Tears began to well in my eyes.

In front of me, was a photo and wooden plaque of "Giorgia," born in July of 2016. A family member with a group of six barrels called a *batteria*—all lined up with her name imprinted on them. Each family member has several barrels which are strictly theirs for the rest of their lives. Marcello explained the process and how only one liter of what the Italians call *black gold* is taken from the final barrel in the line—the oldest barrel, each year. Can you believe it… only one liter? About one liter of new cooked grapes gets added to the newest barrel; subsequently, one liter from the next in line is moved until it reaches the oldest barrel in succession. The fermenting liquids are transferred from barrel to barrel.

The handling of grapes is very different in winemaking versus balsamic vinegar. The term "cooked grapes" refers to the reduction of grapes that are literally cooked in the production of true traditional balsamic vinegar. The reduction of these pressed grapes results in, "*mosto cotto,*" known as cooked grapes.

As we looked around the room, I saw other family names engraved on other barrels. Marcello pointed out the row of small barrels for his children, nieces, and nephews. It's not about money. This family takes care of its own through tradition, quality, and passion. I inconspicuously wipe the tears from my cheeks.

From this room, we entered a smaller room where barrel successions are from his great-grandparents and grandparents. I could barely hold it together. Thank goodness it was time to taste test, I would have time to compose myself. We all took our seats in the original room with the long table. Gary and I took seats opposite our friends. Paolo and Marcello brought in the gastronomic delights. Huge boards filled with local prosciutto, various salamis, and olives are available for each couple to share. Baskets with assorted artisan breads were also on the table. Next, two small whole wheels of different aged Parmesan arrived at the table to sample and were left for everyone to enjoy.

The balsamic tasting began. Marcello explained the difference between what you might buy in a grocery store and true quality balsamic. This widely popular condiment has been copied and reproduced by many countries but true balsamic comes from Modena. He explained the meanings of IGP and DOP and how these products are regulated by the Consortium. The information and history are fascinating. With our small ceramic spoons raised, a few drops of sixteen-year-old balsamic vinegar was distributed for us to taste. Shortly after, the thirty-five-year-old and even one hundred sixty-two-year-old balsamic is distributed for tasting. The extremely old vinegar is from his great-grandparents. I told Marcello he was crazy for sharing—perhaps I wouldn't be so nice. He smiled.

We tasted everything, including some balsamic condiments laced with tartufo and their balsamic called Saba which they use for salad dressing, fused with quince apples. We even dressed our strawberries with a drizzle of balsamic. All this while enjoying their own Lambrusco red wine. More than content, we couldn't eat another bite. Gary and I quietly chatted about what we wanted to buy and noticed Giacomo already standing at the register placing his order. I told Marcello how much this tour meant to me, and that we would do a post on our blog about it. Gianna and Giacomo were right—this place is very special, and I can see why they would bring people here for the experience. Packing the car with our purchases, this experience is worth every *centesimi,* penny. As we drove out of the parking lot, Marcello and Paolo waved back.

ଓ

Planning a reunion with our mi.o friends, Peggy, and Frank, currently in Narni, Italy, they decided to visit us in Lucca this year and stay overnight. We were excited to see them again, although, I see Peggy most Saturday nights Zooming in language class. Gary and I started thinking of where we wanted to take them to dinner. They've visited Lucca before, but quite a few years ago.

Just a day before they arrived, I woke up and informed Gary I'm coming down with a cold. I can feel the congestion in my head. A summer cold—the worst. I spent the day on the couch drinking lots of liquids and taking vitamin C in hopes of nailing this bug instead of falling victim to it. I put some essential oils in the diffuser, but by the evening, I'm worse.

"I'm not gonna pull ahead on this one," I mumbled to Gary.

The next morning, I couldn't bring myself to swing my legs out of bed. I became extremely weak and puzzled. After listening to Frank's voice message, they were arriving a little earlier than I thought they might be since they were traveling about four hours by train. I texted Frank that I was a little under the weather and Gary would meet them at their Airbnb at about eleven o'clock for a short walking tour. Sleeping most of the day, I woke to Gary telling me about their lunch and tour. He made reservations at Vinarkia for drinks at six-thirty and we would meet them there.

I forced myself to dress, but I thought if I stayed an arm's length away, I'd be all right—they'd be all right. I couldn't imagine them coming all the way to Lucca and not seeing them to catch up, as we enjoyed our adventure with them in Grosseto last year so very much.

Thinking it might be wise, we sat outside. Nicola took drink orders. Telling him I wasn't feeling well, I ordered something non-alcoholic. He decided he was going to make me something with some fresh ginger and fruits. It's delicious, as are all his drink creations, but I wasn't feeling the social scene. Several friends passed by, and it was all I could do to hold up a hand and acknowledge them with a wave. Just by chance, our friends Gianna and Giacomo were here to enjoy dinner and paused to meet our friends as they arrived. After about an hour, I needed to call it a night. Both Peggy and Frank understood, but still—they came all this way.

The next day I grew worse. Since Gary was headed to the pharmacy, to pick up his normal medications, I asked him to pick up a COVID home test for me. We hadn't needed to test before, so I didn't order any online before this moment. I'm sure it was a head cold but… you never know. We texted Frank apologizing that we wouldn't be able to see them before they boarded the train back to Narni. We'd make plans to meet again later this year.

ଓ

You guessed it. My COVID test came back with a positive result. After all this time avoiding the virus—I caught it. The worst part of the whole thing? In our tiny three-room apartment, how would I isolate from Gary? Besides, he'd already been exposed. We also immediately texted Frank to let him know my results and how sorry I was for meeting them, but I had no clue my being under the weather had been anything more than just a cold. They appreciated the heads up and we were very happy to hear they did not wind up catching it from us that evening.

After showing some symptoms, Gary decided to test himself. His two home tests showed "invalid," so a few days later he headed to the pharmacy, for an official test. He texted me that he's "positive." So, in our three little rooms, we recovered together. You know we always do things together, why would COVID be any different?

୨ Massarosa ୧

It was that time of year again—time for the celebration of flowers blooming in the nearby town of Massarosa. Last year at the end of June, Gianna took me on a drive to see the gorgeous lotus flower field. We enjoyed an amazing day but if you recall, we never did find the lavender field nearby.

This year, Giacomo decided to take us both for a leisurely tour. He remembered where each of the fields were located. Plus, it was a beautiful day for a car ride. Gary was a bit under the weather, so I took the opportunity to give him some peace and quiet for a few hours and would enjoy this beauty by myself. Gary's not a big flower guy anyway so I'm not sure he even wanted to go.

During our travel through small winding back roads, we passed an unusual sight. I didn't give it much thought at first, but when we passed another woman sitting under an umbrella, just off the side of the road, Giacomo sees my curious expression from his rear-view mirror.

He looks at me by way of the mirror and says, "You do know what they're selling, Ilene."

"Lemonade?" I replied.

Gianna and Giacomo started to chuckle, and I was completely puzzled, not understanding the joke. I knew I was naive but… soon guessed the correct answer wasn't lemonade.

"They are ladies offering services," says Giacomo putting it as nicely as he can.

I respond at once, "Off the side of the road?"

It was an eye-opening moment and one I never would have expected. Out in the middle of nowhere, there are several of these umbrella stands spaced out along the road. They informed me it's common to see this in Italy. I just shook my head.

ଓ

First stop, the same beautiful lotus field but this year, Gianna timed it perfectly. The farm was open, and we walked down and inside the metal gate surrounding this family's property. Walking along the outskirts of the swampy area, these beautiful, white, and soft pink flowers were magnificent. Observing them so closely this year created a whole new perspective for me. Some of the flowers looking up at them from below, almost seemed translucent in the sunlight. The various stages of the flowers, however, caught my attention. Gianna and I both noticed that many of the flowers appeared to be spent. Already, so early in the season? We're both surprised. Yet, numerous blossoms hadn't even opened their petals. Such an odd comparison. We each took our time walking around the field and taking photographs. The leaves of a lotus flower are quite large, almost round. For some reason, they intrigued me almost as much as the flowers themselves. The variations of green from light to dark captured my attention.

With the conclusion of our photography session and leaving the lower, marshy area, we both stopped, noticing a stand offering assorted items for sale. We both focused on one item in particular that caught our attention. Buckets were filled with tall brown sticks with large circular heads at the top filled with seeds. Anyway, we assumed they were seeds. Gianna inquired in her best Italian, pointing to the pods, asking the attendant what they were. Without saying a word, he pointed to the lotus flowers. Eureka moment! They're dried lotus pods we've appreciated many times before in eye-catching floral arrangements and dried wreaths. Their warm brown color had always been a perfect interesting, added decoration when I created silk or dried arrangements back in the States.

ଓ

From here it was off to find the lavender field, the one that eluded Gianna and me last year despite her determination. Going through dirt roads, Giacomo pulled over and found a spot to park after finding the field easily. Gianna and I shook our heads from side to side as we both recall turning left at this juncture last year rather than heading straight ahead, arriving at their location. We were so close, last year.

The field is lovely, although small compared to photos I've viewed on social media taken close to Pisa. Clumps of lavender in long even rows fill the nearby landscape. In a quiet moment, as I approached the middle of the field, I caught the melody of bees buzzing around me. I paused to be cautious, but they were busy pollinating, and unconcerned with me.

Photos taken, Gianna and I are quite happy we're here. Although, the lavender seemed to be more of a blue-grey, purple than the vivid, strong purple I had been expecting. Nonetheless, we both were content we were able to enjoy it together this year.

☙

On the way back to Lucca, I spotted fields of yellow off the autostrada and mentioned to them how striking the patches appear. Gianna inquires if Giacomo would like to try and find the fields in the distance. With his easy-going nature, he suggested it was a beautiful day and we should try and find them. Doubling back, he takes several small roads in the correct direction. He has an idea where they might be found.

While checking my phone from the back seat, I heard Gianna gasp. Startled, I swiftly looked up and dazzled by the sea of yellow right in front of us. We've reached one of the fields I saw from up on the hill. We are at ground level and the beauty surrounds us.

Gianna and I bolt out of the car. From this dirt road, there are sunflowers with their sizable faces looking at us, while on the other side of the road, they are the complete opposite, their heads are turned away. I took a deep sigh, it's awesome. Sunflowers always bring a smile to my face, and today's no different. We each take off walking along the road snapping photos. The flowers are so close, that I don't even need to use the zoom on my phone. I glance over and catch Gianna's huge smile. I smile back and wink.

⸙ Marina di Pisa ⸙

A surprise text message from Pepper and Rusty inquires if we can arrange a free day to take an excursion with them. These two have become good friends following one of those chance meetings. Originally from Little Rock, Arkansas, these are the same two we met for lunch when our chef friend, Margie, was visiting us before heading back home to the States after her Sicilian adventure. They own a charming bed and breakfast in the town of Ghivizzano in the Lucca province. They were "between guests" and bore some time available.

We decided to enjoy dinner in Marina di Pisa, an area of Pisa we'd never been to before. Rusty suggested we make a few sightseeing stops while on the way to this town on the Ligurian Sea. With Rusty driving, we took a leisurely drive, catching up with each other as we hadn't met since Christmastime. We enjoy hearing about their guests and the trips they take with them. From their photos on social media, they go out of their way to make each customer feel special.

The day was glorious and when we arrived later in Marina di Pisa—the skies were a light blue, scattered with thin white clouds. The contrast to the deep blue color of the ocean was striking. Restaurants, pizzerias, and bars lined the seafront and pedestrian walkway of Via Maiorca. The opposite side of the road has a long pebble beach with calm waters from the stone barriers found offshore. What's unusual about this walkway, are the extremely large boulders, chunks of white marble, separating the pavement to the beach. Pepper pointed out cruise ships off in the distance, south of us in the town of Livorno. This is the port where our friend Joanie had been docked with her husband earlier in the year.

Strolling along the walkway, we caught up with our lives—life for them in the mountains, and for us in Lucca Centro. We found a place and enjoyed an *aperitivo* and stopped at a favorite restaurant for dinner. They made reservations so we are seated right away at an outside table. The menu boasts some amazing seafood dishes, and we placed our order just as the sun began to set in the sky. The original light blue color developed into a darker blue and the sunset changed it even more to various shades of purple and bright orange. I excused myself to step away and take a few photos.

As I arrived back at the table, our waiter brought over several orata arranged on a silver platter. We each made our choice of this small but delicious white fish. Rusty and I chose to grill our selection, while Gary ordered his baked. Pepper doesn't care for seafood, so his dinner selections were quite a bit different than ours. He's sweet to allow us to enjoy seafood.

Both Gary and I enjoyed the entire day, and we couldn't thank these two more. It was well after midnight before we returned home. We enjoy our get-togethers when they pop into Lucca Centro to visit or on days like this.

Volterra Winery

Gary

Our morning ritual goes something like this—we wake up and open all the windows to let in the fresh air. One of us will make the *caffè*, then Ilene checks email from our blog or book followers, and scans through our social media. Sometimes Ilene will call me to read a comment a follower has left us, or she will just read it aloud for me to hear. After all, on opposite sides of the apartment, we are no more than twenty steps away.

Today, I'm in the kitchen making *caffè* when Ilene called to me to come see an email. It looked like an invitation from the marketing manager of a vineyard, MonteRosola. We hadn't heard of them but were intrigued. Now mind you we don't know every vineyard in Italy, but it seemed odd to both of us we'd receive an invitation to attend a free wine tasting with a light lunch and tour of the vineyard. Ilene assumed it was a spam email and almost deleted it. When we looked on the Internet, we were both very surprised.

It looked like a resort—not what your typical vineyard looks like, and it looked brand new. With our interest peaked, Ilene decided she'd contact Sharon, the marketing manager, and find out a little more about MonteRosola. It seems Sharon has followed our blog for a few years now, and knows quite a bit about our journey and our move to Lucca. We told Sharon we didn't own a car, but that we have two friends who both entertain a passion for wine and could drive us. She advised they had room for two more.

We immediately called Gianna and Giacomo to explain the whole situation and they both said they'd love to take us there and join in the day's festivities. Giacomo is a bit surprised at the invitation. He's been to quite a few vineyards throughout Italy but has never been invited to attend a festivity like this one.

He said, "It pays to have famous friends," and we all laughed.

With everyone in agreement, we confirmed with Sharon and graciously accepted her invitation. The highly anticipated day arrived for us to visit MonteRosola for our wine tasting and tour. We met Gianna and Giacomo at their apartment, climbed into their Mini Cooper, and took off on our adventure. Giacomo decided to take a scenic route through the *bellissimo*, beautiful Tuscan countryside. Ilene and I love meandering through this region with its small winding roads, gorgeous villas, vineyards, and olive orchards.

As we reached our destination, Ilene is surprised and realized we'd been in front of MonteRosola before. She recognized the gigantic metal oval sculpture on the hill before you enter the main building. On a tour a few months ago, Giovanni stopped at this same gate and told us about the vineyard and the beautiful structure and new owners. I remember saying to Ilene how gorgeous the property looked and that we'd need to come to visit it one day. Well, today's the day—and we didn't make the connection until now.

While we waited for the gates to open, four more cars arrived. Once opened, we all slowly drove through the winding gravel road past the huge art piece and were finally greeted by our hostess, Sharon. She led us to the beautiful reception area within the compound where delicious glasses of white wine were distributed to all of us.

Sharon informed us that not only is MonteRosola a winery but was built as a destination spot. They plan to host weddings, birthdays, meetings, and other similar events. We all followed Sharon to the winery where the magic happens.

Room after room was set up specifically for touring. Large glass windows strategically placed between rooms let you capture the full picture. Their tasting room was impressive. Attractive terracotta tiles adorned the floor in a herringbone pattern while the walls displayed deep, rich wood and stone. Four individual large U-shaped bars occupied the four corners of the room. Each bar was set up with everything one would need to do a proper tasting.

On our next stop, we learned where the grapes are sorted from the stems and seeds, pressure squeezed to remove the juice, and sent to the proper vat where fermentation occurs. They don't crush the grapes as conventional wineries do. The grapes enter a large cylinder with a large pressure bladder, and as the bladder fills with air, the grapes are squeezed until they surrender their wonderful juice to make their wines. It's a process I'd never seen before, but it makes perfect sense to squeeze the grapes slowly instead of crushing them.

Arriving at the rooftop terrazzo, we were able to take in the views of the entire vineyard. A small vineyard existed before the current owners bought the property. Like everything else in Italy, the owners needed to obtain permission from the local government to expand and build the new winery. Once permission was granted, they started expanding the vineyards by moving tons of volcanic soil and blending it with existing earth to acquire the drainage and nutrients their vineyard would need. As we surveyed the entire estate, we could see where new sections showed signs of being prepped and expanded even more.

We transitioned to a gorgeous room where the table was set for lunch. The dim lights in the dining room allowed the table to first catch your attention upon entry. The table was extremely long and narrow, while highlighted with an under-surface light running through the center. Each place setting offered five wine glasses along with the place settings for our lunch. The wine glasses were already poured and positioned perfectly on the lighted part of the table for a dramatic effect. It's a sight to behold, beautifully done, and very pleasing to the eye.

Lunch was served and the sommelier who gave the tour, and the winemaker, started telling us about each wine he poured and how to pair it with food. In all, we enjoyed three reds and two whites along with a charcuterie of meats and cheeses. I would be remiss if I neglected to tell you about the people who shared our afternoon adventure.

Ten of us sat in total. Gianna and Giacomo you already know, two young ladies either both or one a sommelier. A journalist, and three very amiable gentlemen from a restaurant in San Gimignano. The older of the three, the owner and head chef of the restaurant, along with two younger employees, also chefs. Each of the three boasted great personalities and were a lot of fun to talk to. Each understood English to some degree, enough to understand us somewhat. Gianna, Giacomo, Ilene, and I would try to converse in Italian, and I must say we did well. As usual, if we mispronounced a word or two, they were more than happy to help us learn.

We all grew quite fond of our new friends, and I believe they enjoyed the afternoon as well. We agreed and decided we need to visit them at their restaurant. Giovanni, the owner asked if we could come in October. It seems they were extremely busy now and wouldn't have the time to sit and talk with us. Business slows down during this month, and he believed it would be the best time to continue and become better acquainted. Giacomo took one of his business cards and we agreed to see them in October. I keep reminding myself it's the people you meet along the journey—that *make* the journey.

We all went down to the reception room to taste one more wine, grappa, and a *caffè* before we left and of course, both Giacomo and I bought some of their wines. The property was beautiful, the wines are young but very good, and the people are friendly and helpful. I've been to a few (that's an understatement) vineyards in Italy, and I can say without reservation, that MonteRosola is a destination we will go back to again.

☙

On the way back to Lucca in the afternoon, a quick stop at our favorite place, Beconcini Winery in San Miniato needed to be made. It's approximately thirty-five minutes according to Google Maps and since both Giacomo and I were out of our favorite Tempranillo wine, we added Beconcini to our day trip.

Ilene called ahead to let Eva and Leonardo know we would be briefly stopping by to do some shopping and as always, they're happy to oblige. We've become good friends with Eva and

Leonardo since we met them last September at their Tempranillo Festival.

When we arrived, Eva is always genuinely happy to see us. A stop at their vineyard consists of a glass or two of wine, something to nibble on, and a lot of conversation. Leonardo was busy bottling wine but stopped by to greet us. Ilene and Eva discussed the upcoming festival which will be on the first weekend of September. We were keeping our fingers crossed we don't encounter any airline problems returning from Arizona since we are to return home to Italy at the end of August. We would be devastated to miss this year's festival. Especially with two couples coming from Arizona specifically to enjoy it with us.

Ilene informed Eva we've approximately fifteen people interested in attending this year and the two couples from Arizona. We mentioned there's the possibility of adding a few more people which brought a big smile to her face. She told us we are confirmed for our table in the vineyard and more if needed.

After what seemed to be a few hours, I reminded Eva we were here to buy more wine. We all headed to the storage building, filled our orders, and said our goodbyes. There are not many times when I buy more wine than Giacomo, but it seems every time we go to Beconcini I do just that. Go figure. All in all, another wonderful day. We made new friends, greeted old friends, and spent the day with Gianna and Giacomo, our best friends.

Fourth of July

Ilene

With July arriving, Gary and I decided to celebrate the Fourth of July, American style. Our good friends Barbara and Tom sent us a box a while back with some red, white, and blue decorations. Everything from balloons, plates, napkins, scarves, and two funky headbands for Gianna and me. We invited a few friends who weren't attending an "American" celebration event at a nearby villa. We kept the attendee numbers low and reveled in hamburgers, hot dogs, bratwurst, ribs, corn on the cob, and macaroni salad. Your typical American barbeque feast. Dessert consisted of blueberries and strawberries served with vanilla gelato keeping with the American color. *Dolce* also included watermelon and my homemade apple pie which paired perfectly with the gelato. The menu couldn't have been better.

During the day, we enjoyed catching up with our friends and one of the cutest moments occurred with our British friend, Andrea. She had no idea what to expect at an American barbeque and was curious about the history of the holiday. It's fun informing her about why the day is celebrated in the States. She's so appreciative of being included on the guest list, even though she's not an American.

Once again Joel was able to join us, along with our neighbor across our street, Candice. Gianna and Giacomo, Andrea, and Theresa, or "Mama T" as she likes to be called also attended. We had the good fortune of meeting Theresa last year when she visited Lucca. An amazing older woman who stole our hearts—including Gary's. She travels back and forth from northern California to Lucca as often as she can. She's remarkable and a true representation of a strong, independent woman. She has a heart of gold and is a complete pleasure to be around, and has become one of our very special friends.

We only met Theresa at the end of her stay last year, but I cried when she left. She enjoys an amazing, interesting past with a famous husband, and we love listening to her intriguing stories. This year, we were blessed to meet two of her children, Renee and Mark. What a delight. We've been able to do a few adventures together with Theresa besides just enjoying Lucca. Theresa will soon leave again, and it will break my heart, but I know she will return, and we will enjoy more time together. Our door's always open to her and her family.

Ilene's Apple Tart

Tools Needed:
9" Tart Pan
NOTE: You can use premade pie crust or make mine an hour before baking

Pie Crust
Ingredients: Important - measure exactly!
2½ cups all-purpose flour, plus more for dusting
½ tablespoon granulated sugar
½ teaspoon salt
½ pound cold unsalted butter (2 sticks)
7 tablespoons ice water

Directions:
1. Place flour, sugar, and salt into the bowl of a food processor and pulse a few times to combine. You could also use a pastry cutter.
2. Add cold diced butter and pulse until mixture resembles coarse crumbs. The mixture should be dry and powdery.
3. Add 6 tablespoons of ice water and pulse until small balls form. Test dough with fingers to make sure it sticks together. If it does, you've added enough water, don't add too much or the dough will be difficult to roll out. If not, add the last tablespoon.
4. Transfer to a clean work surface and gather dough together in a ball. No need to knead.
5. Divide in half and flatten each ball into two disks. Wrap each with plastic wrap and refrigerate for one hour.

NOTE: I like to blind-bake my bottom crust, so it doesn't get soggy. You don't have to do this step, but I prefer it this way. Here are those directions after you've made the dough and waited at least one hour:

Blind Baking:

1. Preheat oven to 350º
2. Prepare a pie plate by coating each nook and cranny with a little butter.
3. Dust the work surface with flour and roll out the bottom crust to about a 12" diameter circle. Wrap it around the rolling pin to transfer to the pie plate. Form the dough to the pan and up the sides to the top of the fluted edge of the pan. I tend to like the sides of the crust a little thicker.
4. Dock the dough by using a fork and make several indents in the bottom of the crust as well as up the sides. Don't worry about making too many holes. This keeps the dough from puffing up while baking.
5. Place a piece of parchment paper on the dough in the pan.
6. Add a bag or two of raw beans or rice to bake with the dough to keep it from rising. This is called blind baking. Place the pan in the center of the oven and bake for about 15-20 minutes. Don't let it brown.
7. Remove from oven and dump beans or rice into a bowl to cool. You can save these ingredients in a Ziplock bag to reuse them again.
8. Let the bottom crust cool while you continue prepping the filling.

Apple Filling

Prep - 30 minutes
Cook - 1 hour

Ingredients:

7-8 granny smith apples, peeled, cored, and thinly sliced
½ cup unsalted butter
3 tablespoons all-purpose flour
1½ teaspoons cinnamon (or more if you prefer)
½ cup sugar
½ cup packed brown sugar
¼ cup water
1 9" double-crust pie pastry, homemade or prepackaged
1 egg plus 1 tablespoon water for egg wash before baking

Directions:

1. Preheat oven to 425°
2. Melt butter in a saucepan over medium heat. Whisk in flour and simmer one minute. Add sugar and water and bring to a boil. Reduce heat to low and simmer 3-5 minutes whisking frequently. Remove from heat.
3. In a large bowl, add sauce to prepared apples. Add cinnamon and toss to coat.
4. Placed apple mixture into bottom of pie plate filling to form a mound. You can add the mixture to the prebaked bottom crust from blind-baking or one just rolled out, your choice.
5. Roll out the remaining circle of dough in plenty of flour to about a 10" circle and cut into eight 1" strips.
6. Lay 4 pastry strips (dusting off any extra flour) vertically and evenly spaced over the top of the filled pie using longer strips in the center and shorter at the edges. Fold the first and third strips off the pie so you can place the remaining strips in the opposite direction and create a weaved pattern.
7. Trim excess dough at edges as necessary and pinch to seal.
8. Brush with egg wash. Place a sheet of foil on rack below pie to catch any potential drips.

9. Bake in preheated oven for 15 minutes. Reduce temperature to 350° and continue to bake until apples are soft, and the mixture is bubbling, about 35-45 minutes.
10. Rest at room temperature 1 hour before serving.
11. Serve with vanilla ice cream and a smile.

☙

With the celebration of the Fourth of July also comes my birthday. This year it was a bit special as I turned sixty-five. Wow… Medicare age in the States. Once again, where has the time gone? I told Gary I didn't want a big celebration but would rather enjoy drinks with a few special friends.

Meeting at Vinarkia, Gary and I walked into their secret garden in the back of the bar. Gianna and Giacomo were waiting for us along with their friend Bill. Pink balloons and a lovely flower bouquet dressed the table. I'm speechless and brought my right hand to my heart. Theresa, and our good friend Betta, from Brazil, also joined the festivities. We clinked glasses in celebration and enjoyed catching up. Two delicious cakes were brought to the table adorned with tall, thin candles. This entitled me to make two wishes.

Betta handed me a small box. I told her we don't exchange gifts, but she insisted. Betta had been aware of this book and its title before most. She thought the title was very special and it moved her. When I opened the box, it contained a beautiful necklace with three hearts. Made from recycled aluminum pots and bottle caps, she bought it from one of her favorite shops in Lucca. It was her words that meant the world to me. When she saw the necklace, she thought of our book title and our hearts finding their home. You know I cried. Later she left me a beautiful voice message…

> "We are always becoming something else. Toward the end of our lives, we can become a beautiful heart. It's all about transformation. We are always reinventing ourselves, especially all of us here in Lucca—trying to restart our lives in a new way" *(Betta, July 2022)*

⸙ Beach Days ⸙

Last year we were so busy with setting up the apartment, the summer passed us by. This year I wanted it to be different. I wanted to experience going to a beach in Italy. After all, we're only a twenty-minute train ride to Viareggio.

Theresa expressed her desire to go too as she's also never been. We planned with several friends to spend the day at the beach and take the bus rather than the train. The E1 or E2 bus from Lucca to Viareggio lets you off right at the promenade, unlike the train that's about a twenty-to-thirty-minute walk to arrive at the water. It's also a pleasant hour ride through some small stops along the way. Our good friend Diana's favorite beach club revealed availability, so we booked it for five people. In Viareggio, I'm not aware of any public beaches. You need to use one of the beach clubs with their various colored umbrellas and lounge chairs all lined up in perfect rows.

Each of these beach clubs is slightly different. Some offer pools and restaurants, while others just a changing room and a bar. I'm curious to see what they're all about. We split the cost of a cabana and enjoyed the day relaxing. The water is clear and just slightly chilly when first getting yourself wet. The small rolling waves and the sandy beach are simply delightful. We all gathered about waist height in the water, relaxing and chatting. I watched small children making sandcastles along the shoreline under the watchful eye of their parents and took it all in.

After lunch, the skies grew dark, and I could hear thunder off in the distance over the mountains. Some in our group thought it might be the sound of waves crashing, but the color of the sky and the winds picking up said differently. It was a great first day at the beach, and one I won't forget. It had been nice enjoying the soft but very hot sand between my toes once again. Memories of going to Tobay Beach on Long Island with my parents overcame me and brought a small smile to my face.

ଔ

Just a few days later, Lita and Guy arrived back in Lucca, and they were interested in going to the beach for the day. Gary didn't want to go on "girls' day," which I understood, but agreed to go with the two of them, even though he doesn't enjoy the beach very much.

Driving to an area found more toward Pisa, we find there are no available parking spots for the public beach. Giving up, we decide to start calling some beach clubs in Viareggio and head north. This time we wound up in a different club than I attended with the girls a few days before. After securing an umbrella and chairs, Lita and I headed directly for the water. It's a clear, sunny day and sunscreen's a must. We talked and enjoyed the water and before becoming prunes, we decided to head back to the umbrella. The day was great and the lunch at a nearby restaurant was over-the-top delicious.

I'd forgotten how much the sun, wind, and water take out of you on beach days. By the time Gary and I made it home, we were exhausted. And still… the day wasn't over quite yet. Lita heard about a Jazz and wine event happening in Montecarlo the same evening. Along with Gianna, Giacomo, Suzanne, and Marcus, we all met in this small town for dinner.

This small town we've mentioned previously is charming. Sitting high up on the hill, the views are breathtaking. After a nice dinner, we walked over to the church to catch some of the music and wine. Small white lights adorned the streets, hung loosely from side to side, creating an enchanting atmosphere.

The stage is outside the back of the church under the stars and bright moon. Approximately 150 people sat in white plastic chairs and our group quietly snuck in and joined them. The music was quite good, even for someone like me who isn't fond of the genre. Though it was more on a "pop style" than a "blues jazz." Enjoying the music with some great wine completed the evening. Events like this happen everywhere in Tuscany during the summer. We were all grateful to Lita for finding out about this one.

❧ Puccini Festival 2022 ❧

Events are posted everywhere on social media and it's difficult to keep track of them all. When I see one, I usually take a screenshot with my phone to ask Gary about it later in the day. The Lucca Summer Music Festival was in full swing in Piazza Napoleone. It's also the middle of July and the start of the Puccini Festival.

Gary and I have gone to several operas in Italy, but all of them by composer Giuseppe Verdi. This year, we wanted to attend at least one of Puccini's operas since he was born in Lucca. There are many events throughout Lucca in honor of Puccini. The 2022 Puccini Festival is our midsummer dream. Since 1930 many of his operas are enjoyed at the lakeside stage built for this purpose in the town of Torre del Lago.

Purchasing our tickets early, we both decided to attend the opera, *Madama Butterfly*. Without transportation, we booked with a local tour company, Tau Touring just for the transportation, and we were surprised the fees were so reasonable.

The evening arrived and we were excited. Even though Italy's been experiencing a record heat wave, we dressed up to attend. Gary even went so far as to buy an Italian-made sports jacket tailored to accommodate his few extra pounds around the middle. The attractive medium blue lightweight jacket looked amazing on him. After buying it, he came home and informed me that it cost more than his first car. He needed a nice jacket for this event, and the upcoming wedding we are attending.

Arriving at Torre del Lago, the vast Lake Massaciuccoli created a beautiful backdrop to the stage, although mostly hidden by trees. The open-air grand theater has a capacity of 3,400 seats in a natural setting just a few steps away from the Villa Mausoleo where Giacomo Puccini lived and composed his music. This is the only festival in the world dedicated to the composer which attracts thousands of people each year.

Our friends Gianna and Giacomo also attended opening night. After finding them amongst the crowds, we took a few photographs of each other, as well as together. We found a table and enjoyed a glass of wine before the performance. I must say, we all looked amazing and although some people were dressed very casually, we looked great.

We parted ways and found our seats. Because it happened to be the opening night of the season, it didn't begin on time. Several dignitaries gave speeches, some words we understood just a little. Finally, the lights went out, and the opera began.

The evening remained quite warm but occasionally, you felt a slight breeze from the lake. The moon was out, and a few stars were visible in the night sky. As usual, both Italian and English words appeared on monitors on both sides of the stage. During the three-hour performance, the plastic seats weren't very comfortable, and I found myself fidgeting a bit.

I honestly liked the performance but found myself comparing it to the three Giuseppe Verdi operas we've enjoyed in Italy. Gary and I discussed this comparison on the way home. Verdi's operas seem livelier and perhaps that's because we chose this particular Puccini opera, *who knows?* We decided we'd attend another during next year's festival and make our final verdict. The evening was wonderful, yet long. It was after two o'clock in the morning before we arrived home and crashed for the night.

~ The Future ~

Ilene

Sometime last year while eating dinner in Vinarkia with Gianna and Giacomo, Rebecca and Nicola approached our table one night while the bar remained relatively quiet. It was odd to see them both approach us, and come stand at the end of the table together—out of the blue. With schoolkid grins, they wanted to ask all of us a very special question. I could see the excitement in Rebecca's eyes, and I glanced over at Gianna with a slight head tilt and a questioning look. *What might they want to ask us? All four of us?* I sat up a little straighter.

Rebecca inquired, "Would you all like to come to our wedding on the eighth of August?"

We all exploded in unison with loud "yes and *si,* of course!"

I noticed that Nicola had a bit of a grin on his face, and it looked like he was happy with our reactions. This young couple had scheduled their wedding before COVID hit. Once the pandemic happened, and with their new bar just opening, they postponed it temporarily. We're all honored at their request and the focus of our discussion instantly turned to… *what does a true Italian wedding look like? What does one wear?*

I glanced over at Gary and told him we were going to delay our trip back to Arizona a few days to accommodate the day of the wedding. There's no way we're going to miss this event. Our current plans involved spending the entire month of August in Arizona. I know what you're thinking… Arizona—in August? The hottest month of the year to visit Arizona—why would we do this to ourselves? Melanie, Gary's oldest daughter was turning the big 5-0, fifty and we wanted to celebrate with her and the family. Her husband, Jerry, was planning a surprise party and we knew we had to attend.

☙

In the months and years ahead, we are looking forward to exploring Europe. As we've mentioned, traveling throughout the European Union is an easy hop, skip, and jump from Italy. We have several destinations on our list and hope you will join us on social media to see them for yourselves. Living in Europe will certainly present many opportunities.

☙

At the beginning of this book, we mentioned when we decided on coming to Lucca that it would make a great "home base" and easy access to a region we have yet to visit, Piedmont. This region of Italy borders France and Switzerland sitting at the foot of the Alps. It's known for its sophisticated cuisine, and red wines such as Barolo, Nebbiolo, and Barbaresco.

As it turns out, we are planning an eight-day trip with Gianna and Giacomo at the beginning of October to experience these wines, and guess what else? Yes… it will be truffle season. We'll be visiting vineyards for wine tasting and truffle events. Gianna is an amazing trip planner and while we've been busy with the publication of this manuscript, she's organized this trip single-handedly, well, perhaps with a little help from her husband. This will be an amazing season to be exploring this new region for us. Stay tuned for lots of pictures.

☙

We will continue to work on the Italian language, and although we enjoy our many ex-pat friends in Lucca, speaking more Italian is something we really would like to accomplish. School will begin again in October, and we will enjoy reuniting with our former classmates.

☙

The return trip to Arizona in August is going to take some finessing. We'll leave after the wedding, but we must arrive back in Italy before the first weekend in September for the 2022 Tempranillo Festival at our favorite place, Beconcini Winery in San Miniato. This leaves us a little over two weeks back in the States to visit family now in Arizona, Nevada, and Colorado, as well as all our friends we haven't seen for almost two years. I hope it's enough time to scoop up and enjoy the grandchildren as much as we can and catch up on all the little stories they want to share with us. Especially the little ones. You know there's always a story to tell.

At least our friends Susan and Ed are planning their trip to Italy, and we've coordinated part of their stay to take part in the wine festival. We met this wonderful couple first in Orvieto and became great friends. They are about thirty minutes or so from Melanie and Jerry's house where we usually stay. We still want to see them in Arizona along with all the friends they've introduced us to, but it will be nice to spend time with them when they're here in Italy.

As it turns out, another couple, Kris and Pete, who were introduced to us by Susan and Ed, were going to come to Lucca and the Tempranillo Festival. They are a wonderful couple, and we enjoy their company. We've all sat around their clubhouse in Verrado, a master-planned community located in Buckeye about twenty-five miles west of downtown Phoenix. It's a gorgeous community at the base of the White Tank Mountains. More than once, we've sat and talked about Italy—imagining all of us enjoying Italy together. Unfortunately, we recently learned Pete is experiencing some health issues and they won't be able to journey to Italy this year. A night under the stars, sitting in our favorite vineyard, enjoying exceptionally good food and wine will sadly be enjoyed without the two of them this year. This evening will include, however, several good friends from our English Monday group, along with Gianna, Giacomo, Susan, and Ed. We will fully enjoy the event as several of us are staying overnight at the same hotel. Acquaintances we met in Italy are now friends whom we'll enjoy again—coming full circle. It's these types of friendships that truly enrich our lives. We are fortunate to be so blessed.

The other wonderful thing we are looking forward to at the festival is finally meeting Laura and Paul from Volterra. If you recall, they were our first connection with this amazing winery with the introduction to their friends, Eva and Leonardo. We will always be grateful to them and to finally meet them at the festival after all these years of corresponding after Paul read our first book. We had hoped to meet them in their other home, Phoenix one of these days but to meet in Italy—priceless.

☙

We will sort it all out and coordinate, I have no doubt. The airlines are still canceling and rescheduling our flights. We've heard there's a shortage of staff and we presume they are also trying to consolidate flights, even though travel has begun to open up. The main problem appears to be flying out of the Pisa airport, as flights are limited. To use our points from last year, we will make whatever concessions are necessary to use them and be done with it. Hopefully, this situation will resolve shortly.

There's one deep troubling thought for me. It's weighing heavily on my mind. When we return to Arizona, will we feel like we're home? It's still our homeland, place of birth, and country. How exactly will I feel? There are so many things happening right now in the States that are disappointing to both of us—politically and economically, but we won't delve into this matter.

There will always be struggles in Italy. Don't be fooled that living in Italy is all *"la dolce vita."* Rest assured this statement is far from the truth. We've persevered through all the adjustments and conditions, from the bureaucracy to obtain citizenship, to learning the customs and practices of a new country. You must have a somewhat strong demeanor to want to live here.

Occasionally, I think about all our single female friends, and how sometimes they struggle—alone. At least Gary and I have each other, and are in this adventure as equal partners. We both want to live here. Italy has a way of transforming you. Yes, we miss our grandchildren terribly and it's always a struggle for us, but we made this decision together for this stage in our lives. We've declared Lucca the "perfect Italian town" for us. It's where our heart has found its home.

Our Favorite Hangouts

Gary

Everybody has their favorite places to go whether it's a restaurant, a bar, a park, or the mall. Wherever it is, it's your spot to hang out. It gives each of us that certain something we desire, a sense of belonging or simply put, a comfort zone.

Growing up in Maspeth, New York was no different from any other city. I learned about welcoming favorite places as a child by watching my family. For example, my uncle Tony, who lived next door to my grandparents, loved his favorite bar—his watering hole as he put it—and would only patronize that specific establishment. My grandfather, whom we called Jaja, would only frequent *his* favorite bar around the corner from my Uncle Tony's. My other two uncles, also living in the neighborhood, each hung out at their favorite taverns. All these bars were located within a few hundred yards of each other. What made their bar different from the others? I've no clue. The beer itself wasn't the issue because all the brothers drank the same, Ballentine Ale. They all enjoyed the same taste in whiskey, Four Roses, and each bar served the same food bought from the same vendors. What was different about each of these taverns for each of them—to choose different places rather than hang out altogether? To this day I believe it was about their comfort zone. Each one had their friends and liked hanging out with them. Of course, Ilene and I have our favorite places here in Lucca where we feel extremely comfortable—where we meet with friends to talk, laugh, share a meal, or just enjoy a good time.

ᴕ

When it comes to food in Italy—the all-important Italian pastime—every once in a while, you just don't want pizza or pasta. We tried a sushi place inside the wall which wasn't too bad. We've gone with a group from Tuscan Wanderers to Pisa to an amazing Mexican restaurant. The food and margaritas are quite good, and this comes from someone who lived in Phoenix, Arizona for thirty-plus years. We've even traveled as a group to Prato to enjoy an evening of Chinese cuisine. So, there's quite a variety of cuisine to be found in Italy.

Mara Meo

There's a restaurant just around the corner from us in Piazza San Francesco called Mara Meo. The first time we went there the manager Samuel came to our table to introduce himself and told us if we needed anything to let him know. They serve hamburgers, sandwiches, salads, and pasta, which are all good. Their pizza isn't the best, but decent. Ilene's favorite is the pulled pork sandwich and french fries. My favorite—the pork ribs. Yes, barbeque pork ribs. My beverage of choice at this restaurant is a Forst beer, *rosso*, red. I enjoy sitting with a liter much to Ilene's amazement.

What I like most about Mara Meo is the way we are greeted by the staff. I like the fact we're known there—we are comfortable there. If I do not order a liter of beer the waitress will ask me if I'm all right. Here's a funny story. One day we met a friend at their *café*/bar across the piazza from the restaurant for an *aperitivo.* It's all part of the same restaurant, just one side of the piazza is their more informal version. It's a warm day, so I ordered a nice cold liter of beer. The waiter informs me they don't carry a liter size.

As he said this, one of the waitresses from the restaurant across the piazza walked by and tells him, "Oh, Gary always has a liter of beer," and she went back across the piazza to bring a liter mug for me.

Good customer service is knowing your customers, and going above and beyond for them. If we walk in during the busy season without a reservation, they somehow always find a table for us. The other evening Ilene had a hankering for a pizza, wings, and a beer for dinner and didn't want to walk far. Completely agreeing on the menu, we headed down the Fosso, the street in front of our apartment, to Mara Meo for our pizza and beer. As we were seated by a new waitress working there, our favorite waitress Julia walked by, then pointed to me, and said, "Gary likes a cold liter of Forst *rosso"* giving her a heads up I guess, but tonight I just wanted a medium-size beer and ordered it. Shortly after our beverages arrived, Julia walked by our table, stopped, looked at my medium size beer, and asked if I was okay. I smiled and told her I was fine; she nodded and continued with her activities. Once again, our comfort zone… we're in our comfort zone enjoying a meal in one of our favorite places.

Vinarkia

Our favorite bar to frequent—hands down: Vinarkia. Why you may ask? The answer is very simple. Vinarkia is our "Cheers." You walk in the front door, and you are greeted by Nicola and Rebecca who are the owners, with a big smile and a resounding "Gary" or "Ilene" just like it happened to "Norm" on "Cheers." Even Eduardo, their awesome bartender greets you with a big smile, a nod of the head, and your name.

Nicola's not just the owner; he's also a mixologist extraordinaire. He comes up with some of the best-tasting drinks I've experienced anywhere and puts them on the menu as well as the standard fare most other bars offer. The man's brilliant. His partner and soon-to-be wife, Rebecca, runs the food and service side of the business and she's wonderful at what she does. She always greets you with a warm, genuine smile. Together they are truly a dynamic duo.

I'd be remiss if I did not mention the food at Vinarkia. The menu is not large, but I can tell you firsthand whatever you order will be scrumptious. Their menu changes with the seasons, like most restaurants in Italy, but they have a secret weapon other restaurants do not possess. Rebecca's Mom, Gracia. She's the cook, and referring to her this way doesn't do her justice. Just like Nicola's drinks, momma's food creations are innovative and whenever she adds a new dish you know it's going to be delicious.

Vinarkia is more than just a bar. Yes, you are greeted with smiles and hellos, but it's the entire "package" that gives me this comfortable feeling. The bar areas are decorated in classy dark wood with wine shelves over the three tables on your left as you enter. As you enter the garden area, you pass three more cozy tables with a very intimate feeling. The garden area is a beautiful setting with a big tree hanging over it which gives ample shade in the warm sunny months and during the winter, they hang a tarp roof over the seating areas, which helps keep in the heat making it warm and comfortable.

Dining at Vinarkia reminds me of being home. I forget that I'm thousands of miles from my family because Nicola, Rebecca, Edwardo, and Gracia along with our friends, embody our adopted family, our Italian family. Nicola and Rebecca bought Vinarkia just when COVID ravaged Italy. They struggled to stay afloat doing whatever it took to keep the doors open. I'm delighted to say that not only is Vinarkia a successful business, but Nicola and Rebecca plan to marry this August. Ilene and I are invited to share their special day with their families and closest friends. Family… this is the reason why I love going to Vinarkia. I'm with my Italian family.

↜ Osteria da Pasqualino Gubitosa ↝

When we first met Gianna and Giacomo, the first place they pointed out to us while walking around Lucca happened to be Pasquale's restaurant. Although the restaurant was closed at the time, we enjoyed the pleasure of meeting the owner, Pasquale, as he prepared to open later that evening. He was very friendly and genuinely happy to meet us. The fact his restaurant is voted the best in Lucca by Trip Advisor has no bearing on why we go there to eat.

Pasquale's not only the owner of this wonderful establishment but he's also a sommelier. He's elated when he can share some of his wine knowledge with his customers. Often I will ask him his opinion on a wine that I want to order with dinner—and he'll give me a "yea" or "nay." If it's a "nay," he'll bring what he thinks we'll enjoy and then explains his reasons for the choice. He never tries to upsell; he just wants his customers and friends to feel comfortable and enjoy themselves. I love when I order a wine that he hasn't enjoyed in a while, he feels comfortable with us, and he'll bring a glass for himself to enjoy a taste.

Osteria da Pasqualino Gubitosa is the complete, proper name of his restaurant in Lucca Centro and one of our go-to places. If you just mention "Pasquale's" to anyone, they will know which restaurant you're talking about. It's comfortable and friendly, and we feel very much at home there. He's more to us than the owner of a fantastic restaurant. We consider him a good friend.

ঌ Events in Lucca ঌ

Ilene

With the nice weather arriving, many events are being advertised in Lucca. It's almost difficult to keep up with them all. As I mentioned, I take screenshots on my phone when I see something posted on Facebook, just to remember to investigate the event further or discuss it with Gary to see if it's something he'd like to attend. Lucca is abundant in culture, art, and musical events, especially for a city of our size. These are things that endear me to Lucca.

ଓ

There are approximately a dozen music schools located in and around Lucca Centro. Born in Lucca, Giacomo Puccini attended the Pacini School of Music. Puccini gave the world some of its greatest operas like *Madame Butterfly* and *Tosca.* On any given day, you could walk most streets in Lucca and hear music disseminating from open windows. Sometimes students are just playing scales, mostly on key. It's a common occurrence and even sitting on our terrace, someone nearby practices the flute. I've also told you too about our neighbor, the piano man.

ɞ

At any given time, you will find posters in store windows announcing various festivals and concerts. You could fill your calendar almost every day with a different musical event happening in and around Lucca. This year's Summer Music Festival boasts big-name artists from the States such as Justin Bieber, and John Legend, as well as talented Italian singers. One I particularly like is Zucchero.

ɞ

Music… the art of arranging sounds in time through elements of harmony, melody, and rhythm. Music offers a universal cultural aspect connecting all of us. I'm not aware of anyone who doesn't enjoy music. Yes, we all enjoy different types of music, but it's something we all hold in common and appreciate.

ɞ

Lucca's also well known for its love of art. Gary and I explored a Caravaggio exhibition with friends which was excellent and on display for several months in Lucca. Palazzos are filled with art fairs showcasing various arts.

ɞ

Every third weekend of the month, the Antique Market fills several of the piazzas around the *duomo*. There are usually about 230 exhibitors each weekend. We've been fortunate enough to find a few treasures there ourselves.

ɞ

The town of Lucca is an industrial paper area of worldwide importance and has stood this way for centuries. Every two years, Lucca celebrates with the Biennial Art exhibition—the largest in the world. The paper art event is mind-blowing, and I never knew paper mâché could become so beautiful and creative.

ᘓ

On April 27 each year, the city of Lucca celebrates one of their most beloved, Santa Zita. Zita was born in a small village not far from Lucca but employed from the age of twelve as a domestic servant by a prominent Lucchese family. Each day from her apron, she would give leftover bread to the poor. She became a well-known housekeeper and Lucca each year pays homage to the Holy, Patron Saint of Maids by celebrating with flowers. Colorful flowers and plants fill Piazza San Frediano where her body is mummified and on display in a silver and glass casket. During this celebration, Piazza Anfiteatro is filled with flowers and plants to purchase.

Walking into the piazza, I was shocked at the transformation. The variety of roses, petunias, and peonies, in every color you can imagine were on display with various vendors. Cacti, succulents, along with herbs and vegetables appeared scattered through the sea of color. Lemon and orange trees along with anything else you can imagine were available here to purchase—and at amazing prices. Needless to say, I picked up quite a few different flowers and tomato plants for our terrazzo. It took two trips to buy everything I wanted but worth it. I can't wait for next year.

ᘓ

Gianna and I attended the Fashion in Flair event held at the gorgeous Villa Bottini. Over one hundred exhibitors from all over Italy displayed their handcrafted items. Gianna purchased a lovely summer pocketbook while I indulged in a colorful bracelet and a long, multi-colored reversible cashmere cardigan. This particular event is held twice a year. Throughout this book, I have referred to a woman's handbag as a "pocketbook." I realize this is more of a New York slang word but it describes a "purse" or "handbag" a woman may carry.

ᘓ

Nine hundred twenty-eight people in the province of Lucca lost their lives to COVID since the pandemic began. A beautiful night in May was dedicated to these souls. The event was called *"Lucca Abbraccia Lucca"* or "Lucca Embraces Lucca." Five hundred people stood in front of spotlights around the perimeter of the city wall and danced to music specially composed by the students at the Boccherini Institute, an international music school based in Lucca.

We went with Gianna and Giacomo to witness the event and to pay our respects. As usual, the event didn't start on time, but we all wanted to see it, so we waited. While waiting, Giacomo told

us to go stand on one of the lights and he would take a silhouette photo of us. We'd provide our own entertainment while waiting for the group to organize. Gianna's still a bit unstable walking through the tall grass after her total knee replacement surgery and we understood. Gary and I positioned ourselves on the light, projecting our silhouette on *le mura*, the wall outside of Porta Santa Maria. With our hands behind our backs, we kissed while Giacomo snapped a few photos. It turned out so cute.

We never seem to be out and about in the evenings. I'm not sure why we don't participate much in the time-honored Italian tradition of *passeggiata.* The whole town takes part, especially on Sunday evenings and holidays. Why are we not on Via Fillungo? I think it's because we settle in later in the day and have just become a bit lazy. We need to change this.

As we notice people walking and assembling to each assigned light position, Gianna finds the correct radio station the music's being presented. We all waited in anticipation. At about nine-forty-five, the music began and so did the dance routine. Although the music and words were in Italian, they moved me. Tears flowed while I took photos and videos of the event, all while listening to the music on Gianna's phone. As I wiped a tear from my eye, I glanced over at her. She knows me very well by now and gave me a reassuring smile, understanding my feelings. In just over a year, this amazing woman has become such a good friend. She has understood and accepted me, and made me feel like I've known her my entire life. I love how friendships grow and evolve. Gianna's very special. Her husband is too.

☙

One of Gary's favorite events to attend revolves around *vino*, wine. A while ago, we attended an event with a group of friends tasting wines from around *Toscana,* Tuscany. It was a glorious day carrying a wine glass in a pouch around your neck. I started strong, but soon realized that with the number of vendors to taste-test, I would need to pace myself. The entry fee was quite reasonable, and I was surprised at all the selections.

☙

Regarding cuisine, of course, no Italian city would be without food events. Not long ago, we attended a Sicilian Street Food Festival. With music playing, you could visit various vendors and enjoy the gastronomical offerings. *Arancini,* those Italian rice balls stuffed, coated with breadcrumbs, and deep fried tasted pretty good. The seafood Gary and Giacomo enjoyed was decent. Not on our menu to try—is the *tigghiola,* made of lamb intestines, seasoned, wound on a stick, and grilled. The highlight, however, was the cannoli.

☙

Walking down the main shopping street, Via Fillungo, numerous times we've come across a chocolate event. Stalls offer homemade chocolates in every variety and combination you can think of. It's not often I can pass up this indulgence. Even when I declare to Gary that I need to lose a few pounds. When these events come to Piazza San Frediano, you can hear the hum of bees who are also attracted to the sweetness of the chocolate.

☙

With the events happening in Ukraine, a group of amazing women in Lucca organized and coordinated a local fundraiser to raise money for the refugees in Italy. Donations by local businesses and residents to Caritas in Lucca, who oversee the refugees in our town, were substantial. It was a grand affair filled with music and delicious official Ukrainian food prepared by the local, Stravinsky Restaurant. The group exceeded its goal thanks to the generosity of the ex-pat community.

☙

You know how much we love medieval fanfare. Flag throwing is always a favorite but this time we witnessed a competition event. We stood for hours with friends in Piazza Napoleone watching several towns, including a team from Lucca, compete in single and double events. It was a very hot day, and I couldn't imagine how the participants in their velvet costumes could manage in the heat. It's fantastic to watch the coordination of their performances and it became quite evident how much time they must spend practicing.

In fact, on any given day, you will hear drums in the distance and know some event or some celebration is happening in town. Most are posted on social media. Lucca has quite a few Facebook groups you can join.

☙

Lucca is bursting with events and festivals throughout the year. We're selective, as we can't attend them all, but we try not to miss the major festivals. I'm not quite sure how one town can host so many activities and experiences to enrich all our lives. These events I've mentioned are just the icing on the cake. By no means are these the top Lucca events, but just a sample of ones we've attended ourselves. Again, *when your heart finds its home.*

Things We'll Never Get Used To

Don't get us wrong, life in Italy's wonderful. We never thought we would be living in Europe—ever. It's truly a strange feeling knowing we are here, living here permanently in Italy. Nonetheless, some difficulties just can't be overlooked. Some people might not overcome some of these points we're going to make. Perhaps we won't be able to either. For us right now, they are challenges we will try to overcome.

1. Let's talk difficulties. The language barrier's always the first major hurdle to cross. You don't think it's going to be an issue—until it is. For example, when trying to engage in a simple conversation on the telephone, nothing translates easily. It's a ping-pong match going back and forth until some sort of agreement can be made. Once that's accomplished? Most of the time you're not sure it really was understood and hope for the best.

2. For us, trying to reschedule packages delivered when we weren't home becomes a major affair. First trying to understand the little piece of paper they left, and if they will be returning for another delivery automatically. Or

do you need to call to reschedule? When you call and listen to a message and they are speaking ninety miles per hour, it's difficult to figure out what they are saying and if they want you to press one, two, or three. Gary and I've come up with a way to help with this situation. It doesn't always work well, but we play the message on his phone—using Google translate on *my* phone to pick up the conversation, sometimes we can understand… sometimes.

3. While still talking about deliveries, mail distribution's just plain peculiar. Possibly it's just our postman but we've nothing else to compare it to. Regardless of the fact, that our names are on the front of the mailbox, we keep finding other people's mail in our *posta* box. Mind you, not just once in a while—each week there's inevitably someone else's mail residing in the building in our box. If it was junk mail I wouldn't mind, but sometimes it's a delivery notice or telephone bill. Which makes me wonder if ours is being distributed to others too?

4. The Italian bureaucracy is legendary. Truly. The red tape and regulations could wrap around the earth several times and come back to the same starting point. Don't even try to administer any logic to it all—it won't work. Not one little bit. Things become more tangled than a bowl of spaghetti.

5. It blows my mind Italy considers itself environmentally friendly. Well, to some extent anyway. We recycle, but Italians purchase plastic water bottles in large quantities. Bottled water fills the shelves in grocery stores almost as much as the cereal aisle in the States. Natural and frizzante, it's imperative to find a better way for them to understand this crisis.

6. Food controls everything in Italy. There are rules and faux pas for almost every food group. Never will you find butter served with *pane,* bread. You are to use olive oil and there are even conditions associated with its use. When it comes to seafood, never will you see an Italian putting grated cheese on such a delicacy to take away from the taste. The cheese will overpower any seafood and just won't be tolerated. In addition, of course, is the time of day you eat breakfast, lunch, and dinner. The list goes on and on.

7. Next there's the subject of time. When you want to meet an Italian friend at a certain time, advise them it's a half hour earlier. Events that are supposed to begin at a certain time will likely start at least an hour later than planned.

8. There's even an unwritten rule for women wearing sandals. Even if the weather is glorious and warm, you will not find an Italian woman wearing sandals and showing their toes before May.

9. This last item is strictly about Ilene. I'm still not used to living in an apartment building. Most everyone living here speaks Italian. Loud Italian. Although I haven't yet mastered the language, I'm unsure if I really want to know what everyone's saying. Perhaps it's just a conversation, I don't know. Yet, it always comes off as yelling, a lot of loud yelling. I'm just not sure about this close apartment living. Not when I can reach out the window and ask to borrow some *zucchero,* sugar from my first-floor neighbor.

Acknowledgments

When Gary and I talked about a title for this manuscript, we knew we needed to somehow refer to our new home. With our Italian citizenship underway and in full swing, a feeling, a sense overcame us both. I had posted a photo on Facebook, I can't even recall about what. Mary, my former co-worker, and friend from PB Bell commented. She remarked… "When your heart finds its home…" It was at that moment—before words were put to paper, that we had already found the title for this book. It's also our friend Maureen, and another co-worker from my pharmaceutical company, who replied to Mary, "I'd definitely purchase a book with that title." Between them, we knew. The intangible feeling you experience in a location, a sense of peace, joy from loved ones, or an environment where you feel welcome. "Home" isn't easy to define, but you know when you're there. When your heart finds its home. Thank you, ***Mary and Maureen.***

We can't begin to think what life would be like in Lucca without the friendship of ***Gianna and Giacomo.*** From almost the very beginning of this adventure, you've been there by our side. What started as mere acquaintances has blossomed into an amazing friendship, we deeply treasure. You both are caring, kind, generous, and compassionate people and we are better for knowing you. To think it all started from reading a blog post. We are grateful and blessed. A very special thank you to ***Gianna*** for your expertise in formatting, and helping us with all the technical details.

We also would like to thank ***Frank*** for taking the time to review and suggest edits to this manuscript. We can't tell you how much we appreciate and value your time. We met Frank and his wife Sharon after they read our first book and visited Lucca. During lunch, Frank offered to review our manuscript for us. We look forward to continuing our new friendship.

Writing a book is harder than most people think, and more rewarding than we could have ever imagined. Both our books would never have been possible without a very special acknowledgment to our friend, ***Maureen.*** We are eternally grateful for your intensive editing of our manuscript—taking our jumbled words, reworking them, and making complete sense of them. Honestly, we don't know how we could have done this without you. You might be invisible to our readers, but your assistance will be the key to our success. We will always be eternally grateful.

Finally, to ***all the friends*** we've made in and around Lucca who have made this our "perfect Italian town" and home to both our hearts.

Map of Lucca

You can access the city, passing through one of its *sei porte,* six gates; moving clockwise from the north, they are: Porta Santa Maria (1592), Porta San Jacopo (1930), Porta Elisa (1811 dedicated to Elisa Baciocchi), Porta San Pietro (1565), Porta Sant'Anna/Porta Vittorio Emanuele (1910), and Porta San Donato (1629).

Mentions in This Book

Throughout this book we've mentioned several people and places special to us. Here's a quick list for reference in alphabetical order:

Acetaia Cavedoni Balsamic:	Via Guerro di Qua, 2, Modena https://www.acetaiacavedoni.it
Beconcini Winery:	Via Montorzo, 13/A, San Miniato https://www.pietrobeconcini.com
Casa La Pace, Bed & Breakfast, Rusty & Pepper:	www.casalapace.com info@casalapace.com
Dario Cecchini:	Via XX Luglio, 11, Panzano https://www.dariocecchini.com
Drive the Vintage:	https://www.drivethevintage.com
Etta's Bookshop:	Chiasso Barletti, 16, Lucca
Fattoria Carmignari Wines:	Via Cercatoia Alta, 13, Montecarlo https://www.fattoriacarmignani.com
Giovanni Palmieri, driver & guide:	https://www.thetuscanwanderer.com thetuscanwanderer@gmail.com
Grapevine:	https://www.luccagrapevine.com
LuccaNews.org:	https://luccanews.org
Maro Meo San Francesco:	Piazza San Francesco, 17, Lucca
mi.o:	https://www.modernitalian.org
MonteRosola Winery:	https://www.monterosola.com/
MyBelPaese, Kim:	https://mybelpaese.com/

Osteria da Pasqualino Gubitosa:	Via del Moro, 8, Lucca https://www.dapasquale-lucca.com/
Ristorante Belforte:	Viale Alessandro Guidoni, Vernazza, Cinque Terre http://www.ristorantebelforte.it
Urbana Farmstead, Margie:	https://www.urbanafarmstead.net/
Tuccori Mariano Macelleria:	Via Santa Croce, 40, Lucca
2Italia Tour Company:	https://www.2italia.com
Vinarkia della Pavona:	Via Fillungo, 188, Lucca

People We've Met

We apologize we weren't able to share the wonderful stories of every person we met this year. Once acquaintances—now treasured friends. Friends we've made along the way because of reading our book, *Our Italian Journey*, or who discovered our award-winning blog, ouritalianjourney.com.

Here's our list, in no particular order. Our fingers are crossed we haven't forgotten anyone. If we did, please accept our apologies and email us. We can always update and revise this list. Thank you to the following people who've enriched our lives and continue to support our journey through social media comments, emails, and texts. You will always be a part of our lives. We hope we meet again, *a dopo*.

Gianna & Giacomo	Lucca, Italy
Suzanne & Marcus	Long Beach, New York
Bernie & Laura	Highland, Michigan
Dawn & Bob	Warwick, Rhode Island
Margie	Little Rock, Arkansas
Jayne	Carlsbad, California
Sharon & Frank	Sautee, Georgia
Tracy & Phil	Chicago, Illinois
Ana & David	El Cerrito, California
Sophia & Ramu	Chicago, Illinois
Brenda & Garry	Fort Saskatchewan, Alberta, Canada
Ann & Terry	Phoenix, Arizona
Mariana	Miami, Florida
Olga	Miami, Florida
Renee & Larry	Longview, Texas
Gina & Jay	New Orleans, Louisiana
Martha & Frank	East Aurora, New York
Lynn & Sam	La Verne, California
Mike	Kissimmee, Florida
Jennifer & Rick	Lancaster, Ohio
Anita & Leonard	Albuquerque, New Mexico

Wendy & Don	San Diego, California
Beth & George	Delmar, New York
Donna	Tucson, Arizona
Laura & Paul	Phoenix, Arizona/Volterra, Italy
Shari & Roberto	St. George, Utah

Personal Request & Note

May we ask you a favor?

If you liked this book and are willing to spare a few minutes, would you please share your written review on our Amazon page or wherever you purchased it? If you can help us do that, it would mean the absolute world to us.

Please visit Amazon and search for "Ilene and Gary Modica" or go to your 'orders' and you can leave a review through that method. If you purchased on Goodreads, you can leave a review at https://www.goodreads.com/ilenemodica

Thank you *so* much. This helps us get the book into as many hands as possible, encouraging others to create their own journeys!

ᘛ

You can view and fully enjoy color versions of the black and white photos included in this book, as well as, the photos from their first book, on the blog, https://ouritalianjourney.com The higher cost of including color photos, would have made this book unaffordable to many. We hope you understand.

ᘛ

With a slight blend from our small eBook, *Returning to Italy During COVID*, you were able to enjoy this entire next chapter of our journey.

In Memory of

Bill Honohan
1949 - 2022

Though you are no longer with us, you will never be forgotten. Ilene will always hold dear the detail they graduated from the same high school—yet met in Lucca. Our hearts go out to your family. May your memory be forever held in the pages of this book and with your friends here in Lucca.

~ About the Authors ~

Ilene and Gary Modica are residents of Lucca, Italy. They received their dual citizenship through the Jus Sanguinis and Jus Matrimoni process at the end of 2018, and afterward took a one-year journey through Italy, enjoying it as citizens, from November 2018–November 2019 writing their first book, *Our Italian Journey* along the way. This book is available through Amazon, Barns & Noble, and other bookstores.

∞

They hope you will continue to track their journey by following them on social media and subscribing to their blog. They value their subscribers and would love you to join them. The blog supplies more information about them and the places they describe in this book. They offer tips on traveling, recipes, hotel and restaurant recommendations, educational information, along with suggestions on places to visit.

www.pinterest.com/ouritalianjourney
www.instagram.com/italianjourney/
www.facebook.com/ouritalianjourney
www.twitter.com/_italianjourney
(YouTube) https://tinyurl.com/OurItalianJourney
www.sendoutcards.com/u/188663 (amazing greeting cards)